The **Other Side**
Of The **Road**

MANY JOE,
THANKS FOR BEING
A PART OF THE PHILMONT
STORY!
ENJOY!
YIS.

The **Other Side**
Of The **Road**

*"The only
things we keep
permanently
are those we
give away."*

– Waite Phillips

Mark Griffin

Published by the Philmont Staff Association

The Other Side Of The Road.

Copyright © 2009

All photos courtesy of the Philmont Museum except: cover photo by Edward C. "Ted" Woodlock, page 39 by Janet Griffin, and page 48 by Mark Griffin.

Book design by Monarch Design

Published by The Philmont Staff Association

Printed in the United States of America

ISBN 978-1-4276-4379-7

DEDICATION

This project is dedicated to my parents, Bill and Rose Griffin, who brought my sister Jorji – a future Philmont Ranger – and me to Philmont and the Philmont Training Center for the first time in 1971; to Bill Wagner and Barbara Saunders who taught me the value of PTC to volunteers and districts; to Tom Deimler who let me participate in a PTC conference when I was on his staff; to Parvin Bishop and Bill Spice who gave me the opportunity to work at PTC; to the hundreds of PTC staff members who made my summers, and the rest of the year, so special; and to my wife Janet and sons Richard, Robert, and Brian, all of whom worked at Philmont.

Contents

Foreword

I do not believe that Waite Phillips could have imagined in his wildest dreams the impact the gift of his Philmont Ranch to the Boy Scouts of America would have on the lives of so many people.

Philmont has been a life-changing experience for each of the hundreds of thousands of young men and women who have hiked the trails.

However, the operation of the National Volunteer Training Center, a.k.a. PTC, has often gone unnoticed. As the Boy Scouts developed the programs at the ranch, and as they evolved, the questions remained what to do with the Phillips family summer home, the Villa Philmonte.

In their wisdom they made it the cornerstone of the Philmont Training Center. After years of restoration the Villa is a spectacular museum on the National Historic Registry, and PTC is a vital part of the BSA and Philmont.

PTC has had as much or more impact on Scout councils and districts across America as any other entity. Each year hundreds of Scouters and their family members attend training conferences to learn the latest and best new programs and techniques related to all aspects of the Scouting program. These Scouters carry this new information to every corner of the country to train other leaders who in turn pass this knowledge on to the millions of Cub Scouts, Boy Scouts, Venturers, District Committees, Executive Boards, and Commissioner Staffs in these councils.

The effect of the Philmont Training Center on the Boy Scouts of America can never be measured. But without its impact, we would not be able to maintain the same high quality programs we now enjoy.

One day I had the opportunity to walk the grounds of the Villa with Elliot "Chope" Phillips, Waite's son. He said to me during our stroll and conversation "I am sure that Dad would be proud of what has happened to his ranch." I am sure he is.   —

Philmont has impacted well over a million and a half youth, volunteers, family members, staff, and guests since 1938. We can all be proud of the impact it has made, and we must do all we can to be sure that as Scouting enters its second 100 years it remains a valuable, integral part of our heritage – and our future.

Bill Spice - Philmont General Manager, 1993-2000

Introduction

There is no accurate way to determine exactly how many Scouts, Scouters, and family members have been to the Philmont Training Center for the wide variety of programs hosted there by the Boy Scouts of America.

However, it is safe to say that more than 300,000 people have attended a conference or participated in a family program at the Philmont Training Center since 1950. Regardless of the numbers, it is also safe to say that every Scout and every leader in the Boy Scouts of America today has been influenced by someone who has had a Philmont Training Center experience.

William C. Littrell, director of the Philmont ranching department for more than 20 years and Philmont's General Manager from 1973-1976, said: "I would like to say in my opinion it [the Philmont Training Center] is probably the most important phase of the Philmont operation. The experiences during the week spread to councils, and have a direct influence on kids, who come back on this side of the road."

Littrell knew that the Training Center not only had an influence on Scouting in local councils. It also had a role in future attendance of the hiking and camping programs at Philmont. Strong local council programs, led by trained, motivated leaders, keep Scouts involved longer, and interested in high adventure. A Scouter's child who goes to PTC and enjoys the family program very often wants to come back to hike the trails.

Yet even if someone only goes to the Philmont Training Center once and never ventures into the backcountry, the experience in the conferences and the family program has a tremendous impact on that life and, through that life, on countless others.

PTC is so successful because it is one of those proverbial "three-legged stools": Philmont itself, the conference topics, and the family program.

Each "leg" is essential for the overall success, and part of Waite Phillips' vision.

This book is about all of that, the origins and growth of PTC, and the wisdom and generosity of Waite Phillips, Genevieve Phillips, and Chief Scout Executive Arthur A. Schuck who made it all possible.

CHAPTER ONE

A Dream Becomes A Reality

As early as 1930 Oklahoma oilman and philanthropist Waite Phillips had an idea to formally share his Philmont Ranch in the mountains of northern New Mexico with Boy Scouts and their leaders. While he was not directly involved in Scouting, Phillips was familiar with the Scouting movement and the good works Scouts were doing throughout the country. He had allowed Scouts from nearby communities to camp on Philmont and had come to believe that the Boy Scouts of America was an organization that was the best at preparing young men for adulthood. Phillips also believed that as America was becoming more of an industrial society, boys were losing an important connection to nature and the out of doors. He wanted to be sure that boys could enjoy a cattle ranch and the mountains as his son Elliott and Elliott's friends had since he acquired the property in 1922.

After nearly a decade of thought, and over a year of persuading officials of the BSA to accept the gift, in 1938 Phillips gave 35,857 acres of his 300,000-acre ranch to the Boy Scouts of America. The following year the new Philturn Rockymountain Scout Camp became a place for Scouts from all over the nation to participate in a high adventure experience on a real western ranch. In Phillips' words, Philturn would be "a university of the outdoors."

Yet Phillips had more than just Boy Scout camping in mind for Philturn. The enjoyment that his wife Genevieve, whom he had described as a wonderful wife and mother but not a rancher or outdoorswoman, and their daughter Helen Jane had shown during their ranch holidays had

During a 1946 meeting at Philmont, Director of Phillips Properties James Fitch shows a map of the ranch to top BSA professional and volunteer leaders: Chief Scout Executive E. K. Fretwell, Philmont's General Manager Minor Huffman, and national executive board members Frank Weil, Walter Head, E.B. Black, and Frank Hoover.

proven to him that his ranch was not just for rugged adventurers. He also wanted Philturn to be experienced by Scouting leaders and their families.

Phillips thought that Philturn had great potential as a location for the training of volunteer and professional Scout leaders. National Council President Walter Head, a banker and insurance executive from St. Louis who led the BSA from 1926 to 1946, Chief Scout Executive James E. West, and BSA Director of Operations Arthur A. Schuck agreed, and felt that the ranch might someday provide a suitable location for a western version of the training offered at Schiff Scout Reservation in New Jersey.

Brochures promoting the first summer of program at Philturn noted that part of the purpose of the new camp was to provide "facilities for the training for local, regional, and national Scouters, volunteer and professional, in methods and practice of Wilderness Camping."

Though Philturn had no facilities for families, promotional materials

16

mentioned Philturn as a destination for a Scouter's vacation with his family. The plan suggested that Scouters could camp on the property while family members visited nearby attractions and stayed in neighboring towns. The 1940 brochure mentioned the possibility of "Scouter Conferences" as a new Ponil Lodge dining and meeting facility had been completed at the Philturn base camp.

Unfortunately, the waning years of the Depression and a looming war in Europe limited training and conferences at Philturn. But again, the forward-thinking Waite Phillips had more in mind. He was considering a second, much larger gift.

Philmont

Early in 1941 Phillips wrote in his diary about a plan for a Family Corporation, with new son-in-law Bob Hefner handling the Tulsa operations and son Elliott – known to most by the nickname "Chope" – the Philmont Ranch. That plan was short lived. Phillips' daughter Helen Jane's recent marriage to Hefner, her second, was already on the rocks, and Chope had decided to quit the oil business. Waite was unsure of his daughter's future, and unhappy with Chope's decision not to follow him in the oil business. Waite also learned that Chope's wife Virginia was "dissatisfied with ranch life."

Phillips soon added an entry in his diary that his original plan would be cancelled and that he "decided to put into effect a long-time contemplated plan of giving the central improved portion of Philmont Ranch to the Boy Scouts of America with Philtower Building as an endowment." He also determined to sell the rest of the ranch "on account of lack of cooperation of Helen Jane and Elliott."

On October 5, Waite met with the leadership of the BSA in Walter Head's St. Louis office and proposed this second gift. One month later, on December 5, 1941, only two days before Pearl Harbor, he penned a "personal and confidential" letter to Head that has been called the "Gentlemen's Agreement" letter. In this fascinating letter Phillips offers several ideas for the operation of an expanded camp, including reminding

Head of a Philturn idea that would later become the Philmont Trail Crew program. He also asked for the "privilege of selecting the name of 'Philmont Scout Ranch' for the entire acreage, including what is now known as Philturn." The formal gift letter to Head describing the proposed gift was dated December 11, 1941.

On December 18, 1941 the BSA's national executive board met and formally accepted 91,538 additional acres, including Phillips' palatial ranch home, the Villa Philmonte, and his Philtower office building in Tulsa.

James E. West immediately sent a telegram to Phillips expressing his gratitude and a note on the scope of his gift: "May I express my personal happiness and gratitude to you for the magnificent gift you have made to the Boy Scouts of America and express the hope it will bring to you as well as to thousands yes hundreds of thousands of members of the Boy Scouts of America great satisfaction. This is the most outstanding gift of this character not only in the history of Scouting but of any educational or social movement of which I have knowledge."

An announcement of the gifts to Scouts and Scouters throughout America was made in the January 1942 issue of *Scouting*. In the magazine Phillips shared some of his reasons for his generosity. "In viewing conditions today, I am impressed with the responsibility of this generation to adequately train its youth – physically, mentally, and morally – to meet the problems they must face in the future. It is my opinion that nothing can be more valuable to this generation than to enlarge this Scouting program, which develops initiative, self reliance, and dependability. It has always been my belief that the best contribution to that kind of development is by living close to nature and through learning to live in the great out-of-doors. It is also my belief that the romance, history, and traditions of the country in which the ranch is located will contribute much towards perpetuating American idealism and patriotism among boys from all parts of America and it is with these thoughts that I felt impelled to furnish an endowment so that all Boy Scouts and their leaders would have an equal opportunity to participate. To summarize is to say – the proper training of the American boy is today the most urgent duty of the American adult – the Boy Scouts of America has the most efficient plan and organization to do such work – the environment of a well developed Mountain Ranch is the best place to achieve this objective."

A Conference Center

With the additional land and potential facilities for conferences at the Villa, a training center was becoming a more realistic possibility.

But the Villa had only four bedrooms that could be used by the ranch management and four guestrooms for visitors, not nearly enough if Philmont and the "Big House," as the Villa was called, were going to be used for the Scouter conferences Phillips proposed.

To increase the number of beds, in 1942 the BSA erected a bunkhouse in the apple orchard just behind a row of cottonwood trees that marked the eastern end of the Villa lawn. This new building could house 96 men in ten rooms and had a small office on the south end. At times two of the rooms in the Bunkhouse were converted to classrooms so that breakout sessions and smaller groups could meet.

At the same time, the Scouts acted on Phillips' suggestion in a January 1942 letter to Schuck and renovated the servant's quarters in the Villa so that it could serve as an assembly hall and dining room. The removal of interior walls of the servants' quarters and expansion of the kitchen in the Villa was completed so that the Villa could now accommodate over 100 for meals or meetings.

World War II travel restrictions unfortunately limited opportunities to visit Philmont to nearby councils in the BSA's Region 9. Despite the challenges, Philmont's war years' manager Minor Huffman saw the value of training at Philmont and was developing plans for the future.

During Huffman's tenure a formal proposal was made to the Philmont Committee and National Executive Board for the establishment of a training center. Schuck's notes recommended leader training and regional conferences at Philmont, suggested a Philmont Training "degree," and possible year-around use of the facilities. Huffman and his staff also considered the idea of hotel-style housing for families after the war. But this idea was quickly discarded as too expensive to build and maintain to meet the hoped for attendance "of thousands." A tent city was thought to be a more likely solution, someday.

During this period the Villa also gave Philmont one of its enduring symbols of participation: the Black Bull. Dr. Elbert K. Fretwell, the BSA's second Chief Scout Executive, selected a red wool jac-shirt as the "Philmont Shirt" in 1944. As an additional recognition of attendance, he designed a felt black bull emblem for Scouts and leaders to wear on the jac-shirt. The design came from a bull in a tile mosaic at the motor court entrance to the Villa. In the early years the plan was for a Philmont camper to receive the head of the bull the first year at Philmont, the body the second, and the tail the third. Soon the bull became a one-piece emblem for all Philmont program participants, no matter how many times they visited the ranch. A white version of the bull was created by Fretwell and presented to Huffman's wife Dena Mae. Huffman and Fretwell thought this version would be appropriate for ladies that visited the ranch, and both bulls were sold in the Philmont trading posts.

Most training offered at the ranch during the war was conducted by members of the various BSA region staffs. The length, topic, and time of the year of these courses varied. The first training under the leadership of the national council was a finance course in 1943 with 50 Scouters in attendance.

May 1946 saw the first National Camp Leader's Course at Philmont, with 101 participants. However, only an additional 75 people in four other conferences used the facilities that year. The Villa and Bunkhouse facilities were not yet being used to their potential. While there were some signs of what was to come, as Philturn/Philmont neared a decade of program, Phillips' and Schuck's hopes for a national training center were unfulfilled.

Arthur Schuck and The Training Center

Things changed quickly in 1948 when Arthur Schuck was named the Boy Scouts of America's third Chief Scout Executive, the first career professional Scouter to serve in that role. Phillips and Schuck had discussed

Second Chief Scout Executive E.K. Fretwell, Waite Phillips, and third Chief Scout Executive Arthur Schuck salute Scouts during a visit to Philmont. These three men came up with most of the ideas and plans for the operation of PTC.

plans for Philmont for many years and shared a friendship as well as grand ideas for the ranch. Schuck had been Phillips' main contact with the national council but had left to become the council Scout executive in Los Angeles in 1944. Phillips felt that their common interest in the early ideas for the ranch had left the national council as well.

Unlike Fretwell, who came to the role of Chief after serving as a top Scouting volunteer and nationally recognized academic, Schuck not only had that close connection with Phillips and Philmont, he did not have the limitations presented by the war. Also, having served as a professional Scouter since 1917 in local council, regional, and national roles, Schuck understood the real value of a Western National Training Center to a wide range of Scouters.

In letters to the new Chief, Phillips reminded him of their idea of an adult training center at the Villa. He told Schuck that he thought the restoration of the formal training center idea would also be a good way to protect the Villa.

Some, including Phillips, felt that the greatest challenge of getting a training center going was the current ranch management. In letters to Schuck and George Bullock, Philmont's Director of Camping, and in meeting notes, Phillips said that the Villa, which was being used as the general manager's home, had not been well maintained and that the downstairs rooms had become what he called a "staff social hall."

Schuck agreed, and in February 1949, he shared with Phillips that "the dreams we had for utilization of the area as a Scout Leader's Training facility in addition to it being a Scout Camping facility had been practically forgotten. We are going to get into this promptly."

Bullock was familiar with the Phillips family – his first job with the BSA was to implement a program to expand Scouting in Region 9 that was funded by Waite's oldest brother Frank, the founder of Phillips Petroleum – got the message as well and wrote to Phillips to tell him that "greater use of the Villa and Bunkhouse as a training center is scheduled for 1950."

The first step occurred in September 1949 with a Scout executive's conference at the Villa. One purpose of the conference was to show these men the property in the hopes that they would promote future use of the ranch. Phillips wrote upon hearing of the conference, "I am pleased to learn of your forthcoming Philmont conferences next September. You and I have built a great PLANT at Villa Philmonte for adult training purposes and that should be beneficially used."

That first Fellowship Conference included 30 Scout executives and, importantly for the future of the Training Center's program, 18 wives. It was described by one Scout executive as the "richest training experience they had ever had."

True to their word, in 1950 three week-long National Council training conferences were held with a reported attendance of just under 400 Scouters and wives.

Letters that fall from Schuck told Phillips that this could be "the greatest training center in America for volunteer leaders," that he was "looking forward to thousands" of participants each year, and that the center would be an "outstanding contribution to our country." He also envisioned that in the summer months "we should be able to offer diversified courses of interest to volunteers," and he agreed with Phillips that they should include wives and family members because "their cooperation is vital to the volunteer and will pay dividends." He wrote that the BSA was going to allocate between $400,000 and $500,000 to accommodate 350 participants a week at the new Philmont Scout leaders' training facility, and a full slate of conferences was planned for the summer of 1951.

Thanks to the wisdom and perseverance of Waite Phillips and Arthur Schuck, the dream of a Philmont Training Center had finally become a reality.

CHAPTER TWO

The Volunteer Training Center Takes Shape

With the success of the 1950 conferences and the national council's approval of funds to greatly expand the facilities at the Villa Philmonte, the future of the new Scout leaders' training facility at Philmont looked bright. The early '50s would set precedents that would last into the next century.

It was obvious that Philmont and the regions would not be able to handle the facilities, the program, and the conferences alone. George Bullock requested and received help from the most logical source, National Director of Volunteer Training William L. Lawrence. Beginning in 1951 Lawrence and his team took over the management of the conferences, and the Philmont staff handled the facilities and family program.

The new facilities and this partnership allowed Philmont and the National Council to offer an expanded schedule of summer and fall conferences. In contrast to the weekend conferences at Schiff Scout Reservation in New Jersey, Philmont would be offering week-long, Sunday to Saturday training experiences.

Scouting magazine, in its May 1951 issue, promoted "a vacation opportunity combined with some fine training. Scouters coming to these conferences are invited to bring their wives." This was a special feature at Philmont that would make Philmont training different. But in the next issue of *Scouting* an idea that would really make Philmont training unique was announced – every member of the family would be invited.

The renovated Villa servant's quarters was used as a conference room from 1942 to 1997. It is now a museum of the Philmont Ranch and the Phillips family.

Since the Villa bunkhouse was limited to men, Phillips had suggested early on that his old Polo Barns be converted to family housing so that every member of a Scouter's family could come. While that possibility was considered, the desire to have the families closer to the existing facilities and the notion of a "family camping" experience, led to the idea of a large "tent city" in the Villa's apple orchard.

The June/July issue of *Scouting* told Scouters that "here is a chance for a glorious vacation experience for the whole family" and noted that arrangements to accommodate entire families and "attractive recreational opportunities" for women and children would be available at Philmont that summer. It also mentioned that "roomy tents with flies, floors, beds, and wardrobe lockers are supplemented by a central shower house, laundry facilities, etc."

Each conference week would cover a specific area of Scouting. There were weeks for professionals, finance, commissioners, troop leaders, Explorer leaders, and Cub Scout leaders.

Fees for Scouters were $35 for the week. Fees were $30 for wives and daughters over the age of 14. Children aged 5-13 were $15 and 1-4 $5. Boys over 14 were expected to "logically register for some regular Explorer trip" offered by Philmont during the week.

The November 1951 issue of *Scouting* included an article titled "Cub Scouters Pioneer at Philmont." This story included photos of the new Training Center and reported that "During the summer of 1951 a total of 112 men, women and children participated in the first volunteer Cub Scouting Conference at the Philmont Boy Scout Ranch. These fine folks who came from 18 states and Mexico were pioneers in the true sense of the word since they represented Cub Scouting's first venture at the great mountain ranch."

More was on the horizon in 1953. The major construction projects that

Families have been "camping out" in East Tent City since 1951 and South Tent City since 1957.

were approved by the National Executive Board in 1950 were completed or nearing completion. The schedule was changed so that conferences would fit neatly into the two-week vacation typical of the day, with time for travel on both ends. Conferences began with lunch on Wednesday and concluded with breakfast on Tuesday, with Sunday set aside for relaxation and tours. The conference offerings were expanded to include a District Operation conference.

Attendance would grow by nearly 15 percent, with 883 in conferences and a total of 2,333 participants. For the first time, Philmont's Scouter training facility was called the Philmont Volunteer Training Center in *Scouting*.

The basic patterns of operation for the next 60 years of training and program were set in these first four years: the week-long schedule with diverse Scouting topics, an age-specific family program including "Small Fry," a backcountry trek for older boys, the tent cities, a day off in the middle of the week to enjoy Philmont and nearby communities, and evening family activities – including a Western dance.

Expansion

Arthur Schuck had envisioned thousands in training and family programs at Philmont each summer, and made sure the funds were available to build a campus that would accommodate them. He knew that the Training Center needed a larger room than the single Villa room for conference participants and family activities, a dining hall that was not in the same room as the conferences, housing for training faculty, a permanent tent city for families with more facilities, and more family program areas.

A 1954 Philmont Volunteer Training Center brochure titled, "Hi! Scouters – Training for You, Vacation for Your Family," touted the new facilities that would greet the staff and families who arrived that summer.

The largest single addition in the expansion was a new assembly hall, dining hall, and kitchen complex on the south end of the Villa. The new building was connected to the Villa at the Gazebo and faithfully matched the style of Waite Phillips' former home. In addition to accommodating

Waite Phillips and Phillips Properties Manager Ray Bryan during Phillips' last visit to Philmont in 1955.

much larger groups, the Villa meeting room would no longer have to be rearranged constantly for meals and other gatherings.

Additional space for concurrent conferences or breakout sessions was created in the form of a new classroom building south of the Bunkhouse and Office building that could be divided into three smaller classrooms.

Housing needs were met with three duplexes on the lawn behind the Villa for faculty and families, and an expanded tent city with new shower houses – complete with washing machines and kitchen appliances for mothers to prepare food for infants – a playground, and an office and gathering building with a craft lodge and trading post.

A very creative renovation of the Phillips' kennel near the Villa resulted in a new summer residence for special guests of the ranch that was called the Cottage. In the mid-'50s Ray Bryan, the BSA's Director of Phillips' Properties whose office was in the Philtower in Tulsa, and his family stayed here for the summer.

As significant as the 1954 expansion was, the Training Center was growing by leaps and bounds and soon stretched the limits of the new structures. Attendance continued to increase: a reported 13.7 percent in 1954 and 11 percent in 1955. The 1956 season would see 1,316 men in training, with 895 wives and 1,727 children. Another $300,000 was budgeted for construction for the 1957 season.

The 1957 expansion doubled the capacity of the Training Center. A second tent city was erected to the south of the Greensward and a second, much larger dining hall with two serving lines was added to the south end of the Villa Philmonte/Assembly Hall complex.

With two new duplexes for faculty, a new recreation building for "handicrafts, movies, and family parties" near the tent cities, and a Health Lodge to replace the nurse's station in the north end of the Bunkhouse, the campus now surrounded the greensward behind the Villa and extended into the apple orchard on the east and south.

The basic layout and structure of today's Training Center was in place.

CHAPTER THREE

Years Of Growth, Change And Challenge

The year 1960 was a year of milestones for both the Boy Scouts of America and Philmont. The BSA celebrated its 50th Anniversary, Arthur Schuck ended his tenure as Chief Scout Executive, Philmont changed the name of Clear Creek Mountain – at the time Philmont's highest point – to Mount Phillips to honor Waite Phillips, and the Philmont Volunteer Training Center turned 10.

That year's BSA Report to Congress noted that 3,857 people had attended Philmont conferences and family programs. In its first decade the plans that Phillips and Schuck had made "for thousands" had been more than met.

More and more committees and services of the National Council were using the Volunteer Training Center for conferences. There was now training available for almost every adult and boy leader in the BSA, and more and more of them were visiting the ranch each summer.

National organizations that used Scouting to serve youth also saw the possibilities of the Training Center to strengthen their Scouting programs. Some conducted conferences in the "off season" months and others joined the summer schedule to take advantage of the family programs.

In 1963 the Church of Jesus Christ of Latter-day Saints chose the Training Center to conduct a summer conference for their top local and national leaders. Fifty members of local LDS stake presidencies and other church leaders attended this first "Scouting in the Mormon Church"

Conference. At the time the organizers stated that the conferences would be held annually "until all stake presidents have attended."

The mid-1960s saw more expansion of the Training Center conference offerings and facilities. In 1965 a new conference room, new duplexes, and a camp for Boy Scouts along the Urraca Creek near the base of the Tooth of Time Ridge were added to the map. In 1968 the original 1954 classroom building was remodeled and expanded to accommodate the professional National Executive Institutes that would now be held at Philmont in addition to the ones at Schiff. Conference attendance was about the same as it had been in 1967 with 1,277 in 28 conferences, but thanks to the new family facilities and promotion, the overall attendance had grown to 5,478.

The late 1960s and early 70s were years of change in American society and the Boy Scouts of America, so of course things were about to change at Philmont.

The popularity of the Training Center and Philmont as a Scouting vacation, an image promoted extensively by Philmont and in *Scouting*, had

The addition of Dining Hall 2 and South Tent City in 1957 more than doubled PTC's capacity.

begun to overshadow the conferences. Too many of the same Scouters were attending year after year, and were not returning to their councils as trainers. Many attended the conference that fit their vacation schedule rather than the one that fit their Scouting job.

Despite the open invitation process, attendance was actually declining. Some thought that it was because the value of the conferences was not what many of the participants who were there for the right reasons expected. There was a wide range of volunteers in the classroom, many of whom were there just for a vacation and did not – or could not – contribute to the conference.

Within the BSA, training concepts and delivery methods were evolving rapidly, as was the structure of the phases of the Scouting program. The national council began to emphasize local council-based training as opposed to national and regional training. Councils and the Volunteer Training Service realized that they only wanted volunteers at Philmont who would go home and share the information that they learned to improve Scouting in their local councils. They also wanted people who could contribute to the success of the conference with their knowledge and experience. They wanted the "right" Scouters, not just "warm bodies."

Professional Scouters were informed in November 1968 that there would be a "new purpose and operation of the Philmont Training Center." Forms for recommending men for training conferences would be sent to councils and the schedule would no longer be publicly announced. A Scouter would only find out about conferences if he was proposed by his council and received an individual invitation from the Chief Scout Executive for a specific conference. Professionals were told that now "more than ever the Philmont conferences will be train-the-trainer experiences, and consequently should not involve unit leaders."

In the January 1969 *Scouting,* volunteers were told "Philmont training courses will now be aimed mainly at key volunteer leaders who are responsible for training, guiding, and inspiring other district and council Scouters."

Schedules and promotional articles virtually disappeared from the pages

of *Scouting*. But attendance actually started to grow again. As councils listed
the names of their best Scouters, and as those then received a personal invitation from the Chief, the prestige of being invited and attending a conference rose. Having a class that included Scouters that were there for the
right reasons made the conferences more meaningful.

Another challenge faced by the Training Center was that, communica-
tion not being what it is today, as changes in the BSA occurred, the
Scouters at Philmont were often among the first to be informed. The
National Executive Board meeting and the biennial National Council
Meeting were usually held in May, just before the conferences started.
Volunteers were learning about changes approved at these meetings and
returning to councils with information that Scout executives and top coun-
cil volunteers who had not attended the national meeting did not have.

An example was the 1971 introduction of the "Improved Scouting
Program" with skill awards, new rank requirements, new positions, a de-
emphasis of commissioner service, new training concepts, new dark green
uniforms for older Scouts, and a red beret as the new headwear for Scouts.
As volunteers arrived home with new information and photos of these uniforms, they often embarrassed their council leadership who knew nothing
about them and would not get the information until later in the fall.

This led to a backlash in many councils against sending volunteers to
the Training Center, and led to a policy that new information could not be
presented at Philmont until it had been introduced to both the volunteer
and professional leadership of the BSA.

This new information policy also led to some interesting and challenging opportunities for the conference faculty. They were not allowed to
share new information and were at times presenting ideas that would be
out of date within a matter of days. It was both humorous and sad to see a
faculty member who was a member of a team that had developed a new
training plan or program, but who could not talk about or share the new
information.

After hitting a high of 1,487 in 1971, conference attendance dropped to
a post-1954 non-jamboree year low of 1,116 in 1975 and a jamboree year

Tom Deimler and the Gulf Ridge Council staff and volunteers were advocates of summer conferences and "off-season" retreats. They were also among the councils that came up with innovative promotional ideas that spread through the BSA.

low of 1,080 conference participants in 1977.

By now many of the changes that had occurred in Scouting over the past decade were getting another look. One of those was communicating the Training Center schedule with volunteers. Stories about the Philmont Volunteer Training Center schedule returned to the pages of *Scouting* magazine, usually in the form of a short feature preceding a list of the summer's conferences.

Volunteers still had to be invited through their council and be approved by their Scout executive, but awareness of the offerings and increased promotion was necessary to turn around the declining attendance. Scouters were once again encouraged to talk to their council leadership and let them know that they were interested in receiving an invitation to a conference.

Another helpful addition was a season-ending week of professional training conferences conducted by the South Central Region beginning in 1975. These family-included sessions exposed the Training Center to a new generation of professional Scouters – who in turn encouraged their volunteers to attend.

Other than these region training conferences, there had been little professional Scouter training at Philmont, with the exception of a 1968-1970 experiment of PTC-based basic professional training, or National Executive Institutes. The number of professionals outside of the southwest who had ever even been to PTC was declining. For the most part the only professionals in attendance during the main summer sessions at Philmont were on the faculty or in a district Key-3 conference.

In the early '90s a few professionals began to rediscover the potential of the Training Center. Among these was an area director named Bill Spice, and two Scout executives: Tom Deimler and Keith Gallaway. Spice served on the faculty, and Deimler and Gallaway took their council staff and key volunteers to summer conferences. Both Deimler and Gallaway wrote about the experiences in *Pro Speak*, a monthly journal for professional Scouters. All three, and others who understood the value of PTC, shared the many positive aspects of the conferences and encouraged other councils to make similar plans. Later Deimler would become the Director of the BSA's Relationships Division, and Spice and Gallaway would each become the Director of High Adventure and General Manager of Philmont.

Yet while Philmont's camping program was growing, and filled to capacity every summer, Training Center conference attendance in 1993 was the lowest since the decline in the late-70s. Family attendance had experienced a steady 10-year decline and was less than half of what it was in 1984. And the PTC part of the ranch operation was losing money.

In the fall of 1993, Parvin Bishop, the director of the BSA's program group, called a meeting of members of the national executive staff who were responsible for conducting the summer conferences at Philmont. He surprised those in attendance by announcing that he was about to recommend the closing of the Philmont Training Center.

CHAPTER FOUR

PTC Makes A "Comeback"

For those with a long-time association with the Philmont Training Center, Parvin Bishop's announcement that he was closing PTC was a shock, but it was also a call to action.

After the shock wore off a bit, Bishop appointed a task force to figure out what the problems were, and what, if anything, could be done to solve them. He said that he would delay his decision pending the report and actions of the task force.

The task force members included the primary players in the Training Center conferences: Ernest "Tommy" Thomas from Cub Scouting, Earle Peterson from Boy Scouting, Dan Ruth from Council Services, PTC director Forrest McVicar, and much to my surprise, a newer member of the National Staff who had not been one of the conference coordinators, but had an enthusiasm for PTC, associate director of Cub Scouting Mark Griffin. Bishop thought I could look at the problem without the bias of "ownership" and even asked me to chair the task force.

The members started by asking questions of people in local councils and everyone involved in Training Center conferences. It did not take long to discover that there were several factors leading to the decline.

The first issue they discovered was a widespread misconception about PTC attendance. Philmont's high adventure backpacking trek program had begun to see annual capacity summers and multi-year waiting lists. Each year, when reservations for the summer trek schedule filled, the camping department at Philmont would send letters to councils thanking them for their support and informing them — and subsequently their volunteers —

that "Philmont was full." Many professionals in local councils assumed that this meant that all of Philmont was full and stopped encouraging volunteers to apply for conferences.

This belief spread beyond local councils. When a member of the committee met with *Scouting* magazine editor Ernest Doclar, a long time career Scouter and supporter of Philmont, about doing a promotional story, he said that *Scouting* did not do regular PTC feature stories anymore because "Philmont was oversubscribed."

Other than those directly connected to the conferences, it had become apparent that almost everyone in the Boy Scouts of America wrongly assumed that the Philmont Training Center was at capacity every summer.

A second issue was promotion, or the lack of it. The divisions and committees of the national council thought that promotion was the responsibility of the Training Center and local councils. The staff at PTC thought that promotion was the responsibility of the divisions and the local councils. Most local councils had no history of, or idea about, promotion. Basically, everyone was depending on just PTC's reputation for promotion - "everybody knows about Philmont and people will come (or go) because it is Philmont so we don't need to promote."

The task force found that there was actually some intended counter-promotion. During the week at Philmont, conference attendees were welcomed warmly, but were told in a nice way not to come back in future summers. Many in the Scouting hierarchy thought that attending a training conference should be a one-time experience. They remembered the days when people went year after year just to go, instead of going to help strengthen Scouting back home.

It was hoped that Scouters who went to PTC would promote back home, and many of those did – enthusiastically. Since they were about the only source of promotion it created a situation where attendance grew from councils or districts with a good history of attendance, sending their best Scouters, but dropped to zero in those that did not.

The only real source of information about PTC from the National Council was the invitation letter and packet sent to selected Scouters by

PTC with a personalized letter from the Chief Scout Executive. However, that process depended on professionals in the local council. Which turned out to be problem number three.

The invitations and letters were dependent on a local council to suggest the names of Scouters to be placed on the invitation list. The challenge was that outside of the South Central Region, very few local council professionals had ever been to PTC. The task force even discovered that three of the BSA's six regional directors – some of the most tenured professionals in the movement – had never even been to Philmont!

Many councils did not even return their invitation lists because "nobody from our council wants to go." Professionals were saying "no" for their volunteers because of their lack of awareness of the value of and misconceptions about PTC, and for the same reasons, volunteers were no longer requesting to attend a conference.

To be fair, it was noted that the 1993 National Scout Jamboree and the 1992 reorganization of the regions, resulting in the end of the South Central Region and their annual training week, had impacted 1993 attendance. But those only accounted for the steeper decline in 1993, not the trend line.

The task force also compared attendance over the years at PTC with factors such as the price of gas, and inflation and unemployment rates in the nation. They found that there was little, if any, correlation. For example, in the early 80s, when all three indicators were high, attendance was growing. In 1984, a year of high unemployment, attendance was at an all-time high. As the economy improved in the late 80s and early 90s, attendance declined. Scouters would indeed come in "bad" times if they knew the full value of the Training Center, but needed to be encouraged to come in the "good" times too.

Active promotion and communication was the key.

Just as it had been in 1968, the goal of this task force, PTC, and the program group was not just to get bodies to fill the seats, or rather the tents. The goal was to get again more of the "right" Scouters who could and would make a positive impact on their area of Scouting service.

Mark Griffin led the Training Center from 1995 to 2000, and Bill Spice served as Director of High Adventure and Philmont's General Manager from 1993 to 2000.

All involved wanted it to be a little different this time. PTC would not be a secret.

It was agreed that it was time to once again use *Scouting* to share the value of PTC with volunteers. Because of magazine deadlines, and to be able to have an impact on the rapidly approaching 1994 season, the program group placed a two-page advertisement for the Training Center in the January-February 1994 issue. The ad included a schedule and coupon that a Scouter could send to Philmont to get more information about PTC or, with Scout executive approval, actually sign up for a conference.

The national council divisions agreed to increase their promotional efforts by developing new brochures and new conferences that would attract volunteers, and professional interest. In some cases they just changed the title to provide more interest and excitement.

But ultimately, the task force thought that the key was the support of local council professional staffs. Strong support of local council staff members resulted in a team of PTC-trained volunteers who were making a difference in councils, and helping with promotion of PTC.

A survey that PTC Director Forrest McVicar conducted in 1993 had shown that the top influence on attending PTC was the letter from the Chief Scout Executive. With the feeling that PTC was full and by invitation only, respondents shared that they were honored to be suggested by their councils to attend these "elite" conferences. But that did not always work, especially in councils without a PTC tradition.

A strong number two in the survey was "my district executive encouraged me to attend this conference." It was clear that district executives who were aware of what occurred at PTC were the biggest promoters of the conferences. When these local professional Scouters met with and encouraged key volunteer Scouters to attend a specific conference, one that would benefit both the volunteer and the service area, the frequency of attendance increased.

Unfortunately, since the majority of local council executives knew little, if anything, about the Center there was also a need to increase professional Scouters' awareness, as well as a need to stress the advantages of sending more of their best volunteers – volunteers who would return value to the district or council and be a value to the conference. To keep the conferences valuable, it would also be important to help professionals understand the need to discourage attendance by volunteers who would not be a positive asset. PTC was not a place to send a troublemaker in hopes that he or she would change.

The task force also knew that the professionals who had actually been to PTC were able to promote Philmont more effectively. Just looking at the caliber of the names on their invitation lists, and the list of those volunteers that then actually attended from their service areas, made their awareness of the value of the conferences even more obvious. They were able to share the Training Center by relating first-hand experiences.

For this reason it was determined that it would be important to both get more information to professionals and to get more of them to PTC to experience it themselves. John Erickson, the Director of Professional Development, and two members of his staff, Dick Austin and Linda

Hughes, were all were very supportive of the idea, especially Linda who was a former PTC staff member.

As a result, a schedule of regular BSA professional training opportunities was again offered at the ranch. Information about the Center was shared at professional development conferences. Each trainee at the Center for Professional Development was given a postcard and encouraged to list the quality volunteers in his or her service area who should be invited to attend. These lists were sent back to the council Scout executives with a letter encouraging them to add the names to their lists.

With these major efforts underway, the task force and McVicar also took the opportunity to make some changes and corrections to enhance the operation of the Training Center.

The value of the shared experience when professionals attended a Training Center conference with their key volunteers was deemed to be important. Since the structure of the conference week actually allowed more time together than a year of district meetings, a shared PTC experience gave these teams a chance to really get to know each other, and at least in most cases created trust and strong bonds within the professional-volunteer team in those districts. So, the task force proposed more conferences that could be for both volunteers and professionals.

The task force found several successful councils that were doing innovative things that other councils could implement. For example, in the Gulf Ridge Council in Tampa there was a promotional plan that included an annual "Philmont Family Meeting" for everyone on their council's or district's invitation list. During these meetings Scouters who had been to Philmont would talk to Scouters on the invitation list, spouses would talk to spouses, and children would talk to children about what to expect at Philmont. These events would provide information and personal experiences that quite often made it easier for a Scouter to convince his family to join him, or her, on the trip.

Starting in 1994, every PTC conference participant was given a handout with the format of the family meeting plan so that they could do a similar meeting back home.

The Training Center decided that the traditional mid-week beginning and ending of conferences no longer fit into the structure of the typical American vacation. So the schedule was changed to a Monday-Saturday pattern making it possible, at least in theory, to attend and use only one week, or five days, of vacation.

To increase revenue, and to keep from raising participant fees, Bishop agreed to a plan which included ending the practice of a portion of the conference fee going to the division conducting the conference and, for the first time, that faculty would have to pay a fee, about half that of participants, to attend.

McVicar continued his pattern of meeting twice a year in the National Office with all of the conference coordinators and division directors. One meeting was in February to both finalize the details for the upcoming year and to set the schedule for the following year. An October meeting was used as a recap for the summer conferences, to encourage promotion for the new schedule, and discuss tasks for the next few months. These meetings were to ensure, from both sides, that things were on track, and they were held in conjunction with National Council committee meetings when more participants would be present. He also met one-on-one with the coordinators at the Annual National Council Meeting of the BSA and the "Top Hands" meeting for Scout executives. Due to Bishop's "threat" and an increased awareness of the issues, these meetings had renewed enthusiasm and importance.

To enhance the value of the conferences, Bishop encouraged the divisions of the program group to introduce program updates and changes at the now annual spring National Council Meetings rather than at fall Top Hands meetings. The latest concepts and methods could be shared again at Philmont in the summer. Volunteers could attend a conference to get more details and would be able to support the new methods or programs.

Bishop also secured the agreement of the regional directors to monitor and encourage the timely return of invitation lists to PTC from the councils.

Attendance in 1994 rose significantly. There were a lot of factors, but the work of the task force played a major role.

The last few pieces of the task force's effort had to wait until 1996 because fees and budgets for 1994 and 1995 had already been set and published. Since the drop in family attendance had been a major concern, there was a revision in the fee structure for family members to make it more attractive for a Scouter to bring all of his or her family. Fees for conference participants in 1996 went up, but fees for family members were reduced. The overall cost for an average family to attend would be about the same, but the lower costs for each family member made it more attractive. Larger families would actually save money.

To help families make longer-range plans, PTC invitation lists were distributed to councils in August, due back to PTC by October 1, and in the mail back to invitees' homes by Halloween.

The year 1996 also saw another schedule change, back to a full week beginning on Sunday. This change was made because the six-day conference week had reduced conference time more than the divisions and committees wanted, and had cut into the very important family time at Philmont.

Breaking Down "The Wall"

Another challenge that Philmont was facing in the mid-90s was internal communication and attitudes. Over many years an imaginary "wall" had been built up down Highway 21 between the training and camping operations.

There was little interaction among the staff, and being a smaller, less famous part of the ranch operation, with a different mission and schedule, the Training Center was often not included in overall ranch planning. There were even members of the ranch committee that resisted any but the most essential capital projects for the Training Center campus. As a result there had been no significant building projects at PTC between 1968 and 1994. And, those 1968 projects were mostly for the National Executive Institutes.

After the successful 1994 season, Forrest McVicar announced his retirement and Philmont's Director of Program Dave Bates was promoted to be the BSA's Director of Camping and Conservation. Spice and Bishop would need to put a new team in place at Philmont.

They selected Frank Reigelman from the Heart of America Council in Kansas City for Camping, and they selected me for the Training Center.

The new 1995 professional leadership team at Philmont was unique in that all three of us had a shared PTC conference and family program experience. We all understood the role that the Training Center played in the Philmont operation, the Boy Scouts of America, and Waite Phillips' and Arthur Schuck's vision. Most importantly, since Frank and I arrived only a month apart, there were no turf battles. With Bill's leadership and this spirit of cooperation, nearly anything was possible.

We all began a conscious effort to break down barriers between Camping and PTC. We looked at the many ranch departments and made changes in ways that made more sense, at least to us. Spice moved the hosting of Wood Badge training and management of the museums to the Training Center director's responsibility. PTC closed its trading post, in large part to encourage PTC participants to walk over to Camping

The quality family program and conference center support provided by the 1994 and 1995 staffs were a big part of reversing decling attendance trends.

Headquarters to see what was going on over there on their way to the store.

The goal was also to have one Philmont staff regardless of where someone worked. During the summer the activities staff planned staff events on days when the PTC staff did not have evening program commitments, or even over at PTC, so that they could attend. Staff members were encouraged to cross the road and eat at either dining hall, and all staff were invited to PTC's Tuesday night Buffalo Bar-b-que.

Spice encouraged the Camping and PTC management to talk to each other, a lot. We traveled around the nation, and once even to Mexico, to recruit staff and promote the Philmont programs, all of them, not just the ones that were our direct responsibility. These changes, real and cosmetic, brought the ranch and the staff together.

Success

While some did not take it seriously at the time, years later Bishop and Spice would say that the "threat" of closing PTC in 1993 was indeed real and actually being considered. When it was made they both hoped that the threat would force all involved to use their best thinking to save PTC. It worked.

The success of this new wave of cooperation, communication, and promotion helped. PTC attendance increased through the remaining years of the century to new highs. By 1998 the facilities at the Philmont Training Center were in use throughout the year. Most importantly, conference attendance during the 50th anniversary summer of 2000 was the highest to date with 6,198 participants, nearly doubling 1993's total of 3,157.

PTC Enters Its Seventh Decade

As the Philmont Training Center completed sixty summers of conferences, family program, and service to the Boy Scouts of America in 2009, it continued to be a vibrant part of the overall training and leadership development effort of the BSA. While attendance declined slightly from the historic highs of the fiftieth anniversary summer, each summer's attendance remained well above the lows of the early 90s.

To promote the conferences and encourage attendance, PTC adopted an electronic invitation and registration process to spread the word directly to more Scouters and added a PTC Masters Track "square knot" for uniform wear. At the same time the National Council of the BSA appointed a task force of top volunteers to look at promotion and the future delivery of conferences at the Training Center.

As with everything in life, there is no telling what the future will be for the Philmont Training Center. Changes in the economy and transportation, new conference facilities at other locations, and changes in the Boy Scouts of America itself will paint that picture.

Whatever the future brings, the real keys to the success of the Philmont Training Center over its first sixty years have always been having the best Scouters, with their families; participating in a quality conference and family program; under the leadership of a top-notch faculty and staff; combined with the beauty of Philmont. When all those things happen, and as those Scouters make Scouting better in their communities and spread the word of the magic of Philmont, the vision of Waite Phillips and Arthur Schuck is realized.

CHAPTER FIVE

Summer Conferences

While they were doing some strategic planning in Tampa in the early '90s, Scout executive Tom Deimler and his staff researched the common traits in their most successful districts. They found something that was the case in districts and councils all over America: a common ingredient in their very best districts was the presence of several dedicated volunteers who had been to a conference at the Philmont Training Center.

Nearly all of the conferences over the years have provided a forum for learning that is unique in the BSA. Being able to spend an entire week of sharing ideas with people from throughout the nation – with your family – is rare in Scouting. Scouters can gain a much better understanding of a part of Scouting, and by participating in a PTC conference gain perspective of the "bigger picture" of the movement.

Since 1951, the summer conferences at the Training Center have been cooperative efforts between Philmont and the staffs and committees of the national council. The Training Center hosts the conference and provides facilities, family program, and support. The national committee determines what conferences are offered, provides the conference content, materials, and the conference facilitators – or faculty as they are called at PTC.

In the early years of summer conferences, at first because there was only one classroom at the Villa, there was only one large conference each week. The first summer, 1950, there were three week-long sessions, one each for commissioners, troop leaders, and Explorer leaders. In 1951 Cub Scouting joined the schedule and there were a total of six summer sessions.

The 1952 Cub Scouting conferences started a pattern of participants choosing a "major" topic of interest in Cub Scouting such as crafts, game leadership, puppetry, pack administration, or the "knack of leadership." These smaller groups met throughout the week with "minor" topics on some afternoons. Each major group was led by a member of the Cub Scouting Service and members of the National Cub Scout Committee.

Cub Scouting was ahead of its time as another unusual feature of the 1952 Cub Scouting Conference was the first inclusion of women in the classroom. As *Scouting* put it in January, "Those wives who are interested in Cub Scouting may join in the conference sessions" and that it was "possible for both mothers and dad to participate."

As the Training Center added classrooms and the Scouting program evolved, the other national council services or divisions began to offer several separate conferences, each related to the division's role. The week still might have been called "Boy Scouting Week" or "Relationships Week" but the conference would include several different topics and no joint sessions. Some weeks included a mixture of topics to accommodate smaller conferences or divisions.

While Cub Scouting also offered several topics during their conference

Quality conferences, led by expert faculty, with plenty of peer interaction and sharing, are a big part of the Philmont Training Center "Magic."

weeks over the years, they never really left the "one conference with break-outs" plan that they had started with in the early 50s. Each of their weeks had an overall conference chair, started and ended with joint sessions, and usually included at least one day of "round-robin" topics. In 2008 Cub Scouting dropped the separate conferences all together and returned to a single conference with breakouts called the "Cub Scout Extravaganza."

In 2009, with another change in the organization of the National Council, the weeks became more focused on a related topic, such as training or membership, rather than a particular phase of the Scouting program.

In reality it would be easy to offer many of the PTC conference sessions anywhere in the country. Those who do not understand the total PTC concept often ask why there is not more classroom time or evening sessions. While very important, what is taught in a conference room is only part of the overall plan and success of PTC. Plenty of free time for discussion, family time to share the activities and even strengthen the family, and the opportunity to experience as much as possible of the beauty and other opportunities at Philmont, are what makes the conferences as ultimately effective as they have been over the years.

Faculty

PTC has historically called the Scouters that lead the conferences "faculty." This is in part to distinguish them from the seasonal and year-around staff, but also to give them the recognition they deserve for being selected for this important responsibility.

Because the conferences are conducted by the national council, the conference faculty is selected by the various committees and teams of the national council. They are not selected, as some think, by the Training Center.

There are several ways that a Scouter is selected to serve on the faculty of a Philmont Training Center Conference. Most of the faculty members are members of the committees, task forces, and staff of the national council that are responsible for the conference topic throughout the year. In some cases faculty come from successful local councils and are recommended by a council Scout executive. Faculty members usually also need previous Philmont experience before they serve unless they have unusual expertise or are part of a local team that has been selected from a successful council.

Another way to serve on the faculty is to be selected from among the participants in a conference. There is usually a broad range of skills and experience among the Scouters in conferences, some of whom could easily lead the course. Unfortunately, all too often a Scouter is guilty of "campaigning" for a future faculty position during the week, and therefore is usually not recommended. The ones who ought to be in the role are usually obvious in their wisdom, their humility, and their ability to facilitate discussion.

The opportunity for local Scouting leaders to spend a week interacting and sharing with the volunteers and professionals who "wrote the book" is another unique aspect of a Philmont conference. Of course, the converse is also true – the connection with grass roots volunteers is also beneficial for national committee members and staff.

CHAPTER SIX

Family Program

Beautiful country, an expert faculty, and fellowship with volunteers from around the BSA and the world make the Philmont Training Center a superb training experience. But the ingredient that has always made the Training Center unique and special is the family program.

Waite Phillips originally promoted the idea for the family program because his intent was not just to provide a place for Scouts to hike in the mountains. He wanted Philmont to be enjoyed by families just as his family had enjoyed the ranch. As is nearly always the case with a Phillips idea, it was and is innovative and successful.

There is little doubt that Phillips was a visionary. You can tell from his writings that he knew the impact that his ranch could have on Scouts, leaders, the Boy Scouts of America, and families. His ideas proved successful in operation, his persistence made sure that they continued, and his financial generosity made them possible for 70 years – and counting.

Philmont has made or strengthened connections with family and friends, with Scouters, with Scouting, with nature, and with God.

In his landmark 2006 book *Last Child in the Woods*, subtitled "Saving Our Children From Nature-Deficit Disorder," Richard Louv shared the latest research on child development that explained what many have learned hiking Philmont's trails, and what Phillips knew when he gave the Boy Scouts of America this wonderful ranch in the '30s. An outdoor experience and connection to nature, like the one that Scouts and families have at Philmont, has been shown to have a significant long-term impact on a person mentally, emotionally, and spiritually. Louv and others have also

Western Dances, such as this '50s square dance in the new Assembly Hall, have always been part of a family program.

demonstrated the importance of creative play that is so much a part of Scouting and the PTC family program.

Over the years many spouses and children have been apprehensive, or worse, when their Scouter talks them into going to a conference at a Boy Scout camp in Cimarron, New Mexico. To ease the concern somewhat, family program and facilities have been a big part of the promotion of the Training Center in *Scouting* magazine and other materials.

From even before the very first summer conferences in 1950, the idea was that there would not only be Scouting training, but that the conferences would include programs for members of a Scouter's family. There would also be plenty of time for a family to enjoy Philmont together. The goal of the Philmont Training Center was to provide a quality conference experience for Scouters with their families. "With" being the key word.

While the programs for families have evolved over the Training Center's history, the basic patterns that exist today started very early. A day

52

set aside with no classroom time so families could do something together, evening "fun nights" including square dances and a picnic, nature trails, day hikes, horseback rides, crafts, and games were all part of the 1951 program.

As was a program for spouses.

The Spouses Program

Phillips and Arthur Schuck knew that a wife's support was necessary to have the best possible attendance at the Training Center. While today there are husbands as well as wives in the spouse program, the idea is the same. Family support of a Scouter is a big key to success back in the local council – and at home.

The spouses' program has changed the least of all the family programs. The PTC idea has always included days that are full of activity for the Scouter and the other members of the family, so that a spouse could enjoy free time doing a wide variety of things – or nothing – without having to worry about the children or the spouse.

Scouting magazine articles in the 1950s and early 60s titled "We Found

Director of Camping Jack Rhea with PTC family members in the Villa's living room. Rhea served from 1954 to 1962.

Scouting's Heart," "Philmont Honeymoon," "Queen For A Week," "The Family at Philmont," and "Mom Goes To Philmont" were written from a mom's perspective and featured the fun the kids would have – and the fun and relaxation that mom could have while the kids were being cared for by the Philmont staff. Of course, over the years the focus of the articles and the sensibilities changed with the times.

A Scouter trying to talk his wife into a car or train trip to New Mexico in 1953 might get her to read this from April 1953's "Like a Vacation?": "The small fry are taken over and given care, fed lunch, given a rest period and kept occupied all day. The gracious rooms of the Villa Philmonte are open for reading, good talk or just lounging. Shady lawns invite relaxation, and the many miles of good roads on the ranch invite casual sight-seeing. Mom will find so many home conveniences that taking care of the family will be easy. The over-sized tents have inner-spring beds, clothes closet, table, chairs, electric light, and all linens furnished. Automatic washing machines, refrigerators and stoves are available. All of the comforts of home – but no cooking to do, no dishes to wash!"

In the '60s the focus started to stray from "domestic" issues to program and recreation, but still had some of the flavor of the times. February 1962's "Hey Wives! Be Queen for a Week" shared that "the great attraction is Villa Philmonte, the beautiful ranch home built by Mr. and Mrs. Waite Phillips and donated with furnishings intact. The house is open to tours and the game room is a haven for the inevitable bridge sharks who find their way to Philmont. If bridge isn't her game, there are many other activities for the Scouting wife. She can make a tour to the Kit Carson Museum, which is staffed (as is the entire camp) by delightful Explorer-age boys, who really get a charge out of showing off the museum's treasures with appropriate explanations. The artists have plenty to sketch; the photographers have many pictorial treasurers to preserve. There are handicrafts for the handy, nature hikes and horseback riding for the outdoor lovers; historical tours for the history lovers; or just plain woman-type gab fests, which, of course, are the most fun of all. The evenings are always busy with family programs, shows, or dances. On Sunday, following church services, the family can take a picnic lunch to one of the beautiful canyons within the ranch area or visit the Indian writings and diggings at Ponil."

When PTC returned to *Scouting* in the '90s, in an article about her family's trip to Philmont titled "A Family at Philmont," Cathleen Ann Steg wrote about her training conference – and her husband's experience in the spouses program!

Children's Programs

It makes sense in an organization that is based on the Patrol Method that small, age-specific family program groups would be organized and given names.

The only family program that has had the same name for over 50 years, and the first to be named in print, is the Small Fry program. In 1953 *Scouting* magazine called the six year old and under group "Small Fry" and described their activities and schedule.

Phillips' 1950 idea of using the Polo Barns for family housing may have provided the idea for converting the south wing of the barns into a Small Fry Center – complete with a pony ring – in 1956. Each morning the Small Fry were bused over from the Training Center for a full day of play, pony rides, and hopefully naps.

As facilities expanded, the nursery and Small Fry groups were split and the youngest family members in the nursery program moved in to the remodeled Health Lodge building on the Greensward. Now they would not have to ride in the school buses to the Polo Barns and their parents could watch them play in the attached Nursery playground.

In 1994 a new Small Fry Center was built near the Handicraft Lodge. This new building, and the 1995 addition of a nearby pony ring, totally eliminated the need to transport Small Fry away from the Villa area. It provided a location for a quality day of fun for nursery and Small Fry while easing the anxiety of parents watching their young ones leave each day on a school bus.

In the mid-90s Gayle Stanton and Martha Collins, a mother-daughter team from a Boy Scouting family with a day care facility management back-

An age-specific, educational, and fun program for each member of the family has made PTC a special place for Scouting families.

ground, joined the Training Center committee. They provided toys, materials and training for the staff each summer and helped to make the building and program state of the art.

Early on, the boys and girls who were seven to 13 years old enjoyed Philmont in groups called Kit Carson Boys and Kit Carson Girls. However, the broad range of ages proved to be a challenge, and there was a desire to arrange the boys' groups along Scouting program lines. Boys soon logically became Cub Scouts and Boy Scouts.

The argument that Philmont is after all a Boy Scout camp, versus the practical application of a Scouting program in a one-week "provisional" program, has caused the level of direct connection with the Scouting program to increase and decrease over the years. At times there have been structured Scouting programs, and at times the programs were Scouting in name only. Some years the directors have decided to, or been given direction to, make the boys' program groups more like Scouting, or at times staffing challenges or management philosophy has caused them to lessen the connection.

For many years a Training Center Cub Scout pack with dens for each Cub Scout age boy was organized each week. Some summers a Cub Scout day camp was held with most of the group's activities at the Stockade, a camp at the foot of the Tooth of Time that featured an old Western "fort." The challenges of maintaining the Stockade and busing the Cub Scouts to the camp every day ended the program at the Stockade after 1991. The day camp and pack idea ended as well.

After Webelos camping was approved by the national Cub Scout committee, a father-son, and later a parent-son, campout was added to the program. Webelos have camped at Rayado, Badger, Ponil, Rocky Mountain Scout Camp, and even the PTC Nature Trail over the years.

Just as there was a pack, there was also a Training Center troop for Boy Scouts. A Boy Scout camp was built in 1965 to provide a summer camp experience for Boy Scouts attending PTC. Called Camp Urraca, it was on the road to the Stockade at the location of the present Badger Camp. On arrival Boy Scouts were formed into patrols and PTC staff members served as Scoutmasters and assistants. They spent the entire week at the camp and participated in shooting sports, hikes, crafts, and all the non-waterfront fun activities you would expect at a regular Scout camp. The highlight of each week for most Scouts was an ascent of the Tooth of Time, usually up and down the old Stockade Trail.

After the summer of 1971 Camp Urraca was closed and replaced by the new Rocky Mountain Scout Camp. Located just up the road from Camp Urraca, the program was similar to what had been offered at Urraca but the facilities and location were much improved.

In 1992 the Boy Scout camping program was discontinued and Scouts were moved back to the Training Center. Staffing challenges, unfamiliarity among the Scouts in a provisional troop, the increasing number of boys in attendance who were not Scouts, and 10 year-old Boy Scouts who had never camped without mom or dad, were impacting the success of the program. Quite often a "Scout" would be found wandering down the road toward Camping Headquarters on his way to find mom.

As with the demise of the pack, the troop and patrol structure also ended with this change. Scouts still did many of the same activities, including the Tooth of Time hike, but they ate most meals in the PTC dining halls and, except for one "overnighter," stayed in their parents' tents.

Because the Boy Scouts had returned to the tent cities, overall weekly capacity was reduced. When attendance returned to near capacity in the late 1990s, 16 smaller "Boy Scout tents" were added to the tent cities to get the space back for conference attendees and to give the Boy Scout-aged boys at least a semblance of camping out away from mom and dad.

One of the challenges that the Training Center staff faced was rank advancement in the "Scout name" programs. For many years this was not a problem because in Scouting in general, and at camp in particular, advancement was more a result of activity and not the activity. Also, since the program was for 11- to 13-year olds, nearly all participants were still working on the basic Scouting skills back home. At the end of the week, parents could get a detail of the Scout's program and could give the Scout credit if the troop back home agreed.

Early 1970s changes allowed, and for a time required, Scouts who were not yet First Class to earn merit badges. Throughout the BSA the emphasis on rank advancement increased and many parents wanted their Scouts to earn merit badges or have a formal advancement plan in camp. This presented many problems, especially in dealing with the broad range of needs, skills, and experience among the Scouts at Philmont.

PTC needed to follow both practicality and national advancement policy. What they did was pretty much summed up in a statement that appeared in the 1996 Family Guidebook:

Please understand that while our Cub Scout, Webelos, and Boy Scout programs may provide some opportunities for completing advancement requirements, their main intent is to let our Scouts have a fun Philmont experience! The true 'arena' for advancement is in the home, the den, the patrol, or the troop and we do not wish to usurp the parent's, the den leader's or Scoutmaster's role.

Other family programs at PTC were give Spanish names or were named for something or someone in local history. The Kit Carson Girls of the '50s became Muchachas and Senoritas of the '60s. From the '70s to the '80s there were Blancas, Ninas, Muchachas, and Los Jovenes. In the '90s there were Ninas, Chicas, Muchachas, and Los Jovenes. Spouses changed from just "women," to Senoras and Senores.

In the early '70s the names Lobos and Blancas were selected for the programs for six- and seven-year old boys and girls. These names came from the wolves in Ernest Thompson Seton's Northern New Mexico story *Lobo, King of the Currimpaw*. Blancas was dropped after a few years, for reasons ranging from Blanca's sad ending in the story to political correctness, and became Ninas. Beginning in 1994 the Lobos were informally called Tigers to match the age range of the BSA's Tiger Cub program. In 1996 the name Lobos was dropped in favor of Tigers.

When there were small numbers of younger family members during a week, the Lobos/Tigers and Ninas programs were merged and called Nibos and later Amigos.

In 2003 all connection with Scouting programs was removed and the "Spanish" names were changed to Western ranch names. Cub Scout and Boy Scout age programs were changed to Cowpokes, Deputies, Sidewinders, and Trailblazers. Girls became Cowgirls, Ropers, and Mustangs. Spouses became Silverados.

These name changes were made primarily because of the challenges the staff faced with potentially wide ranges of ages in Scouting programs. The age and/or grade program requirements that the BSA programs had adopted, along with the variables of Webelos-to-Scout transition calendars, often created a broad age range within a group. At times there were both 11-year old Webelos and nine-year old Boy Scouts in those groups during the same week. These variables had also increased the movement between family program groups after arrival at PTC. Since it was important for safety reasons to know where a participant was at all times, these last-minute group changes created additional challenges for the staff.

Eliminating the Scouting connection through boys' group names, and

Pony rides have been a popular program for PTC's younger participants. The original ring pictured here was located behind East Tent City and was used until 1956 when the Small Fry moved to their new center at the Polo Barns.

sticking with age-only program groups made things much easier for the PTC staff and more consistent – age wise at least – with the girls' program groups. But there are some traditional thinkers who are saddened by the disconnect with Scouting.

For the first two decades of the Training Center only boys over the age of 14 could go on backcountry treks, and those treks or junior leader training courses were the only choice for teenage boys. Eventually a shorter backcountry trek that matched the PTC schedule was offered for sons – Mountain Men – of conference participants.

Until the '70s, girls of that age – called Senoritas – planned their own program of activities and stayed in tent city. As girls became Explorers and were allowed to serve as Philmont Rangers, Mountain Woman treks were offered.

In the '90s the name for both groups was changed to Mountain Treks.

When older boys started to arrive at Philmont who were not Scouts, or did not have the interest or ability to take part in a trek, a co-ed program called Los Jovenes ("the young ones") was created. Los Jovenes took on the method of the Senoritas and did as much, or as little, as they wanted each week. Quite often they were bored – usually by their own design – and a burden to the staff and parents. In 1996 a Training Center C.O.P.E. (Challenging Outdoor Personal Experience or "ropes") course was built and a string of horses returned to basecamp for PTC program. Those became popular features of the Los Jovenes program and a more structured program became the norm.

The Philmont Training Center family program is not designed to just keep children - and spouses - busy for the week while their Scouter is in a conference. While things may change occasionally due to attendance or a current program manager, the programs have been designed to meet the specific needs and interests of the variety of age groups that come to PTC. In addition to the program possibilities provided by Philmont's other departments, the staff has led family members in nature study, crafts, Scoutcraft skills, field sports, initiative games, Project Wild, and other educational curricula. Of course, just like the backcountry treks, hiking on Philmont's miles of trails and enjoying the beauty of the ranch had always been a key feature of family program.

Every PTC director has stories about Scouters and families at the Training Center. Each week they hear from Scouters whose enthusiasm was renewed or whose families become closer and more supportive because of the Philmont experience. A few years ago a Scouter who had just left the Training Center called on a Saturday morning after they had left the ranch. He said that he had to call as soon as he got a cell phone signal to share his story. As his family had left the parking lot, driving past the Villa and the cottonwoods, his wife thanked him for bringing their family to Philmont. She added, "I will never resent the time you spend in Scouting again."

That is what PTC is really all about and what Waite Phillips had in mind.

CHAPTER SEVEN

Training Center Staff

There are several groups that have worked closely together to make the conferences and family program so successful over the years – the Philmont staff, the Training Center committee, the national committees, and the conference faculty. Each plays an important role in that success.

But, if you ask someone who has served as a director or manager of the Philmont Training Center what the best part of the job is, or was, he will probably tell you working with the young and not-so-young, members of the Training Center seasonal staff.

Each summer hundreds of people, mostly college students, arrive to spend about three months together providing family program and supporting conferences. Their specific responsibilities, leadership, and titles have changed over the years, but the main responsibilities of family program, conference support, tent city management, and food service have been consistent.

For many years the top seasonal staff leader at PTC was called the "Training Center Manager" or the "Family Program Manager." In 1997 as a result of a restructuring of the PTC staff that gave the position more responsibilities, the title was changed to "PTC Program Director." In 2008 the assistant director of the Philmont Training Center took over the management of the program staff.

Today the seasonal Training Center staff consists of family program group leaders, C.O.P.E. staff, handicraft staff, services staff, registration staff, tent city managers, a pony wrangler, and the dining hall staff. Seasonal staff from other ranch departments that support PTC programs include the museum staff, the Mountain Trek rangers, and wranglers.

While most members of the seasonal staff arrive in May and leave in mid-August, there is a small group that stays on for the fall and winter conferences. Depending on the conference, they lead a modified family program and provide nearly all of the other services that the full staff does in the summer.

Like Scouting in general, until the 70s most of the staff at the Training Center was male. The only females were the daughters or wives of other staff members or local residents. Due to the nature of the activities and participants, the Training Center was a natural fit for the first female staff at Philmont – many of whom had participated in the family program with their families and wanted to go back to Philmont.

Today the staff is usually more than half female, and many are former family program participants.

While the seasonal staff at PTC comes from many sources, much of the seasonal staff is recruited on college campuses all over the nation. Philmont staff members, seasonal and year-around, visit schools to inform those looking for summer jobs about Philmont opportunities. Some universities even offer internships and academic credit for the summer.

In the past a Training Center job was usually considered a "stepping stone" to a backcountry job. However, while some start at PTC, and in subsequent years take on a backcountry assignment, in recent years more and more have decided to serve several years on the PTC staff.

From 1950 to 1968 the Training Center facility was managed year around by the same staff that was leading the camping and other programs at Philmont. During the summer one or more of the professionals of the Volunteer Training Service of the National Council would move out to Philmont to manage the conferences, but the family program was managed by a summer seasonal staff member.

As Philmont's overall popularity grew, and with the advent of professional training at the ranch, the BSA decided to place a professional on site with primary responsibility for the Center. The first manager was Darwin Van Gorp in 1968, followed by Will Conradi in 1970.

At the September 1974 ranch committee meeting it was announced that because of a reorganization of the national council, and the loss of the PTC National Executive Institutes, a switch was going to be made back to seasonal management. Once again, as with the other ranch departments, a seasonal staff member was hired and assigned to manage the Training Center staff for the summer.

The first seasonal Training Center Manager after the change was Clyde Clark. Clyde had retired after a long career as a professional Scouter as the National Director of Relationships in 1975, and headed out to the ranch to manage the Philmont side of the Training Center operation. Clyde was well respected by the staff and a constant, enthusiastic promoter of the conferences. Because of his service with the national council he already had a strong relationship with the members of the Volunteer Training Division and was able to effectively coordinate the conferences and the family program. Under Clark's leadership conference attendance at PTC grew from just under 3,000 to over 5,000 participants – during some challenging times for the economy and the BSA. He served in this role until 1984 and had a tremendous impact on the Training Center program and the success of the entire operation.

The second, and last, seasonal PTC manager was long-time Philmont summer staff member Gene Schnell in 1985.

With the growth of the backcountry and training programs at Philmont, the BSA saw that the overall operation of the ranch was becoming too complicated and the Training Center once again needed year-around management. To meet that need, one of the former Volunteer Training Division staff members, Robert Maxfield, became the first to have the title Director of the Philmont Training Center on January 1, 1986.

Maxfield served until his retirement in 1989. Forrest McVicar, who for many years had been associate director of Exploring, led the Center until his 1994 retirement. I had the honor of serving from March 1995 to February 2000.

When I left to become the Scout executive in the Blue Mountain

In 1958, its ninth season, the Philmont Volunteer Training Center was already very successful and required a large staff to serve thousands of participants each summer.

Council based in Kennewick, Washington, Rick Barnes, the Scout executive in Sioux Falls, South Dakota, was selected as the new director. Bob, Forrest, and I had all come from the national staff, so Rick was the first to take the position from outside the national council. After two summers Rick was selected as the new Scout executive for the council in Ogden, Utah, and later Salt Lake City. Brian Gray followed Rick in 2002 after giving leadership to the Maui, Hawai'i council.

With the increase in year around activity, a new year-around professional position was created in February 2008. The new position included the responsibilities of the summer program director and coordination of "off-season" conferences. The first to hold the position of Assistant Director of the Philmont Training Center was Greg Gamewell.

Like all of Scouting, Philmont is governed by a volunteer committee. Philmont's Ranch Committee includes volunteer Scouters and experts in a particular phase of the ranch operation, and makes plans for the ranch and gives direction to the year-around staff.

A sub-committee of the Ranch Committee, the Training Center Committee works with the Training Center director to oversee the program and make recommendations to the other sub-committees regarding facilities and support of conferences.

The Ranch Committee meets at least twice a year, occasionally at one of the other High Adventure bases with the other base committees and/or the National High Adventure Committee. Committee members are also involved with the annual camp visitation conducted by the Boy Scouts of America.

Since they live, eat, and work together all summer, with essentially the same work schedule, the Training Center staff, like backcountry camp staff, develops a strong bond through these shared experiences. Many times I have tried to find a way to put that into words, and failed. In the spring of 2009, former PTC staff member Amber Heide Abercrombie blogged about her Training Center experience. Amber served on the staff as a group leader in 1999 and then in 2000 and 2001 on the COPE staff. She met her husband Mark there. I think that Amber put into words what so many of the staff have felt.

COUNTRY THAT I LOVE

They call it "God's Country." Now, I'm not sure who "they" are, but nothing more perfectly describes the almost 140,000 acres in the Sangre de Cristo Mountains that make up Philmont Scout Ranch. Three of the best summers of my life were spent there. Outside the walls of my own home, it is my favorite place on earth.

I tried, and failed, numerous times since the inception of my blog, to craft a post that would do Philmont justice. I needed you to understand. I needed you to know what I know. I needed you to share the passion. And then I realized I could load a post with the most carefully chosen adjectives, and it would not matter. Because try as you might, you will never "get it." No offense to you. You just can't "know" unless you have stood shoulder to shoulder and swayed to the Philmont Hymn during closing ceremony. You can't understand, unless you have seen the sunrise from the Tooth of Time. And even if you tried to "get it," the language would trip you up.

No, I am aware I won't be able to make you understand how Philmont is just a little bit magic. But it is part of who I am. And so, regardless, I will introduce you.

I had the hand-drawn map, penciled by my uncle (who understands, because he not only landed me the job, but worked there during his younger years), lying in my lap as my trusty pregnant roller skate (a.k.a. a 1991 Geo Metro) puttered down the tree-lined drive. According to the map, I was right where I should be. Yet, I had the desire to turn around and drive the 18 hours back home without a backwards glance. Who was I trying to fool, anyway? Taking a job at a Boy Scout Ranch in Middle of Nowhere, New Mexico to "find myself." Who cared that, four college majors later, I was a dropout and a miserable 9-5 job awaited me back home? My life might have had no direction, but at least back home I wasn't an hour from civilization, pulling up to a strange new job alone. Hopelessly alone.

What had I gotten myself into? I was going to spend 3 months without a blow dryer, living in a tent with a bunch of strange tree-huggers? By choice? Surely any pre-mid-life crisis in Idaho would be better than that.

The map said turn, and so I turned. It was the only thing in my life at that moment providing direction, so I felt it best to abide by it. I pulled up to the offices of PTC, and my life has not been the same since.

Everyone has a story to tell about what defines them. What event altered the course of their life. What experiences led them down the path they are currently on. My life exists as I know it because of Philmont. Snagging a husband aside, it changed everything about who I was and how I viewed the world.

Philmont is pure. She almost demands that you are in return, if you choose to hike her valleys and temporarily seek shelter on her ground. You must drop the facade. Strip yourself of your worldly possessions, throw the curling iron in the back of your brand new car (in fact, leave that parked in the driveway, halfway across the country while you are at it). Wash the make-up off your face, so she can see who you really are. So you can see who you really are.

I arrived with a simple suitcase, and a lifetime full of baggage. I unpacked the suitcase, and the rest unfolded itself.

That summer we rock climbed until our fingers bled, sported killer tan lines (the socks-must-be-worn-with-sandals rule did us in) and ate more squeeze cheese and Apple Brown Bettys than I would like to remember. We forgot that adults have responsibilities in the real world. Bills were foreign to us. TVs and newspapers spouting a week's worth of worldly calamities were ignored, as we spent our time lounging outside of so and so's tent, planning our next adventure. Occasionally, we would dab on a coat of mascara, run a comb through our hair, strap on our Tevas and pile into someone's car to make the one-hour trek into town.

There we would rub our eyes, trying to adjust to that thing they called reality, while stocking up on the finer things in life that the dining hall deprived us of. Namely, Cheetos and chocolate. Then we would marvel at the new songs on the radio, as we drove the windy road back to our canvas paradise.

Sand volleyball on our lunch breaks. The like-clockwork-monsoon-induced rain showers in the afternoon. Piled into the Small Fry building at night, to watch whatever portion of a movie we could keep our eyes open for.

Someone's boxers always wound up hoisted to the top of the flag pole, or someone had to emerge after a shower wearing only a shower curtain when their clothes were "accidentally" misplaced; and a cot-on-the-rooftop retaliation was inevitable. Someone was always dating someone else, and then breaking up with that someone to dump someone else. Someone was always making Dutch oven cobbler. Someone was always putting on their best western attire to line dance the hours away at Western night. Someone was always shirking on their bathroom cleaning responsibilities.

I miss all those someones. I always will. I have never loved a group of people as much as I loved my fellow staffers. The bond was unique, because it was real. All of the shallowness, the competitiveness, the my-dad-is-stronger-than-your-dad antics did not exist. I am not sure why that was. It just was. And I established the truest, most lasting friendships because of it.

This post might not mean much to most of you. But, for those of you who understand that "Waite" was/is a perfectly acceptable man's name, Muchachas RULE, and puke green is the most attractive color around. For those of you who know just when to shout "MOUNTAIN MAMA" at the top of your lungs and how miserable it is to drag a reluctant Boy Scout up the Stockade trail. For those of you who ache for the simplicity of that place. For those of you who know. This is for you.

Thank you Amber!

CHAPTER EIGHT

"Off Season" And Other Training

While the summer Training Center conferences at the Villa complex are the most famous, and the largest in annual attendance, there have been a wide variety of summer and "off season" events held at Philmont over the years.

Executive board retreats, endowment seminars, professional staff conferences, local council training weekends, Order of the Arrow events, National Camp Schools, and of course Wood Badge and junior leader training have all found a place at Philmont. Even NASA came to Philmont in June, 1964 to train astronauts in geology in preparation for the exploration of the Moon! Six of the twelve men to walk on the moon, including the first four (Neil Armstrong, Edwin "Buzz" Aldrin, Charles "Pete" Conrad, and Alan Bean), Apollo 13's James Lovell, and original Mercury astronaut Gordon Cooper were part of a group of 20 in attendance.

Many national organizations and groups that use Scouting to serve youth have held training or conferences at the ranch as well. For example, from 1957 to 1964 Philmont hosted a Tribal Conference for Native American Scouters with representatives from as many as 28 tribes in attendance.

Most of these conferences have been hosted by the Training Center and, while the summer is the busiest time of the year, they have turned PTC into a true year-around operation.

Fall PTC Conferences

In addition to the summer offerings, the 1951 schedule included a November Explorer Leaders' Conference. Late summer and fall conferences were an important part of the early Training Center plan.

When most of the BSA's training was "localized" in the 1970s, fall and winter conferences conducted by the national council pretty much disappeared from the schedule. Other than the PTC office and the Villa, the center's buildings were "winterized" and closed from September to May.

In 1995 National Director of Program Parvin Bishop suggested that there should be more year-around use of the facilities at PTC. Funds were provided so that insulation and heating could be added to most of the buildings, including the duplexes. This increased the potential for hosting more, and larger events. But there was little interest among the national council's divisions in formal conferences.

During the summer sessions in the late '90s the Boy Scout Division had begun to offer more and more outdoor program conferences that wanted to venture into Philmont's backcountry. There was a concern, which often came true, that there might be a conflict between these conferences and the backcountry programs for Scouts in the mountains. Crews of Scouts having a wilderness experience did not necessarily want to see an all-adult crew on the trail. Already overflowing backcountry camps and programs did not need more campers.

These conferences were also very "family unfriendly" since the participants were away from PTC-proper for most of the week. This of course was contrary to the mission and the strength of the Training Center summer conferences.

With expanding school calendars, expanding summer conference attendance, and an interest among the divisions of the national council to have more and more conferences, space was becoming a challenge.

In 1998 John Alline, at the time the director of Boy Scout training and the Boy Scout conference coordinator, and Boy Scout national committee training chair Nathan Rosenberg agreed with a suggestion by the

BSA leaders at the Villa during a visit to Philmont after World War II. National President Walter Head, General Manager Minor Huffman, board member Frank Hoover, and Chief Scout Executive E.K. Fretwell.

Training Center director to move some of their conferences to a new week of program in September in 1999. In addition to the backcountry conferences, it was decided that a couple of Center-based conferences – such as Scouting for the Homeschooled or Teaching Basic Scoutcraft Skills – would be offered at the same time in the PTC classrooms. These conferences would be for both those that wanted to attend a session in the fall, and those who had planned to attend a backcountry conference but did not pass the medical requirements of the backcountry. The fall conferences are much smaller and feature a modified family program so that Scouters can still bring their families.

Professional Training

The Philmont Training Center was and is called the Volunteer Training Center. For many years this was a formal designation, although the word "volunteer" disappeared from most official publications in 1992. Yet the first training conferences at the ranch and the Villa were for career professional Scouters, and professional training has been an important part of the conference schedule for most of the Center's history.

Beginning with a 1943 finance conference and the 1949 Scout Executive's Conference, Philmont offered a western conference setting for the movement's professional leaders well before formalized volunteer training was featured. Every year during PTC's first two decades the conferences included required professional training as well as specialty topics that would be of benefit to career Scouters and councils.

To accommodate the increasing number of men entering professional Scouting, in 1968 the National Council decided to use Philmont as a western location for the National Executive Institute. NEI was the basic professional training that had been offered previously only at Schiff Scout reservation in New Jersey, and was required for a professional to receive his commission. To make this possible, additional classrooms, housing, and other facilities were built at PTC and in Philmont's administration area for the faculty and participants.

In making the announcement of the additional location for NEI, Director of Professional Training Don Fifield stressed that the training would be equal to that conducted at Schiff and that, in addition to instructors from the National Office in New Jersey, top executives and regional staff from the western regions would be used. Fifield noted that participants in the courses would be selected randomly from throughout the nation and it would not be just for Western professionals.

Unfortunately, the experiment was short-lived due to transportation challenges for the participants and the guest instructors visiting from the National Office. By 1971 all of the NEI courses were back at Schiff.

For many years the BSA regions that included Philmont conducted regional professional training, often including a family program element. With the cancellation of a planned national professional training conference in 1975, the South Central Region decided to conduct a week-long session at PTC that included management and finance training, and a full family program. These were basically an extension of the summer conferences and continued until the realignment of the regions in 1993.

Today the Training Center works with the BSA's Center for Professional Development to offer several courses in the spring and summer, and professionals are encouraged to attend other summer and fall offerings.

Junior/Youth Leader Training

On April 15, 1949, Arthur Schuck told Waite Phillips that "we have cooked up a new idea of providing an all-summer training program for 32 carefully selected boy leaders who will train the older boy Unit Leaders in their respective local councils. This is a training project that has great possibilities in its extension and ramifications and in years to come we could give this outdoor training experience to hundreds of boys each summer." Phillips replied giving his "hearty approval" to the idea.

Philmont's first Junior Leader Training Troop was formed in July 1949. In those days Scouts and youth often attended "camp" all summer, so lengthy camp sessions were not unusual. The first course lasted 42 days and had 26 participants. The idea was successful, and only two years later there were eight, 36-day sessions with 32 participants in each session.

The Carson-Maxwell Base Camp, later called Rayado, was the location for most of the advanced Boy Scout and Explorer youth leader training courses until 1994 when they were moved to Rocky Mountain Scout Camp.

From 1976 to 1980 the national youth training courses were discontinued and only local council courses were held. In 1981 a week-long National Instructor Camp resumed at Rayado under the leadership of course director Carl Nelson. In 1982 the course was re-titled National Junior Leader Instructor Camp.

The names of the various youth training courses have changed over the years, the latest being the National Advanced Youth Leadership Experience. Perhaps one of the most interesting of the course names was the 1973 "Woodman's Thong" course.

These training camps have had an evolving content, participant base, and schedule over the years. But all have had the intent of training youth

In July 1949 Philmont hosted its first youth leader training program. These twenty-six Scouts spent 42 days at the ranch.

leaders and helping them pass their skills on to the other youth in their troops, teams, posts or crews.

Wood Badge

The second Wood Badge course offered in the United States was held at Cimarroncito Base Camp (now called the Hunting Lodge) in October 1948. Due to the success of Wood Badge, and in an attempt to give the course a Philmont camp that did not impact other programs, a new Wood Badge Lodge was built at Zastrow Camp for the second Philmont course in 1949. This Zastrow course would become the prototype for courses all over the nation, making Zastrow and Philmont, in the minds of many, the "home" of American Wood Badge.

In 1995 the hosting of Philmont Wood Badge courses was shifted from the camping department at Philmont to the Training Center. Zastrow continued to be the site for national, regional, and local council Wood Badge courses until 2002 when the camp was taken over by the camping operation for use as a mountain biking camp. Since then all Wood Badge courses have been held at Rocky Mountain Scout Camp.

There have been a variety of Wood Badge formats hosted by Philmont. In May of 1996 the Training Center hosted a Cub Scout Trainer Wood Badge conducted by the National Council and led by course director ("Cubmaster") Sue Weierman. Sue was a long-time member of the national Cub Scout committee and frequent member of the PTC faculty. Sue's course was held on the PTC campus. Sessions were held on the lawn, the Greensward, and in the classrooms. "Gilwell Field" was on the front lawn with the Tooth of Time in the background.

Perhaps the most famous, non-traditional Wood Badge format was the "Walking Wood Badge" that was offered from 1976 to 1994 by the South Central Region. The course was similar to the Wood Badge course offered in other locations around the nation, but involved hiking in Philmont's backcountry and emphasized backpacking camping skills. There were many national and regional reasons for the demise of this course, but from a Philmont perspective the increasing load on the backcountry from growing attendance by Scouts was an issue.

In 2000 Philmont was once again the home of a "second" Wood Badge course for the BSA. A new Wood Badge for the 21st Century was first piloted at the Florida Sea Base in January, and that fall the second pilot course was held at Rocky Mountain Scout Camp. Dan Zaccara was the course director for the Philmont course.

Powderhorn

In 1999 the new Venturing program was developing an advanced training program for adult Venture leaders. Under the leadership of the national Venturing committee, and course director Donna Cunningham, the first Venturing "Powderhorn" course was held at the Hunting Lodge and in the Cimarroncito Meadow that September. The pilot course had 50 participants and tested many of the concepts that were included in the final course.

Local Council Conferences

Many councils have held staff conferences, executive board retreats, weekend volunteer training and family events during the "off season" at the Training Center.

The Amarillo, Pueblo, and of course Albuquerque councils have been the most frequent visitors, but local councils all over the nation have been welcomed to hold their own conferences. Multi-council conferences are often held at PTC to take advantage of national council support and the sharing of ideas among volunteers and staff across council lines.

For many years these events were limited by space issues and to the weeks just before and after the summer because of weather and staffing issues. When the duplexes and conference rooms were insulated and heated in the mid-'90s, comfortable, year-around use became possible.

Philmont provides a unique environment, and spirit, for these conferences. The Training Center provides a quality facility for housing, meals and meetings. The Villa Philmonte and the legacy of Waite and Genevieve Phillips provide an example of generosity that quite often helps increase council support.

Of course, part of the goal of these conferences is to give more local council volunteers and professionals a Philmont experience so that they will be able to encourage more Scouts and volunteers to come to Philmont's training and camping programs.

CHAPTER NINE

Philmont Museums

The history of the Cimarron Country was an attraction to Waite Phillips when he bought the ranch, and to Arthur Schuck when it was gifted to the BSA. The lure and excitement of the "Wild West" and the natural history of the area continue to draw people to Northern New Mexico. In an effort to preserve and share as much of this history as possible, Philmont maintains several museums. Some are formal museums, others are historical ranch cabins, homes, or collections of artifacts at backcountry camps. There are three museums that, while not part of the Training Center proper, are closely connected and an integral part of the family program and among the best "free time" activities on the ranch.

The Villa Philmonte

Waite and Genevieve Phillips' ranch home, the Villa Philmonte, was designed by Kansas City architect Edward Buehler Delk and built under the direction of the John Long Construction Company between 1925 and 1927. This team also built, at the same time, the Phillips' home in Tulsa, called Philbrook. Philbrook is now a renowned art museum.

After the Villa was given to the Boy Scouts as part of a 91,538 acre gift from the Phillips family in December 1941, the home was used as a residence, meeting rooms, and a gathering place for Philmont participants and staff. Occasional self-guided tours were conducted.

Beginning in 1976, Elliott "Chope" Phillips and his wife Virginia led an effort to restore the Villa to its pre-1941 condition, including sending the rugs from the Villa to Ireland to be restored. Using a wealth of photographs, and the return of more of the family furniture, the effort brought the home as close as possible to the way it was when the family enjoyed the ranch. The main rooms of the Villa ceased to be used for other purposes and the home became a museum.

That summer Lou Love, a staff member for 25 summers, began the first scheduled tours of the home.

In 1998 the servants' quarters, which had been used as a classroom and dining hall since the 40s, were converted by Villa Superintendent Nancy Klein into a museum of the Phillips family and their years on the ranch.

At the end of the century, after nearly 25 years of hosting thousands of annual visitors and countless tours, it was becoming apparent that the 70-year-old Villa was in need of more repair. In order to make the extensive repairs, and to fund them in a way that did not impact the other capital needs of Philmont, for the first time Philmont embarked on a fundraising campaign. So as not to impact local council fundraising either, the campaign was limited to the Philmont "family" – ranch committee, staff, neighbors, and the Phillips family – and over $2 million was raised.

Beginning in the fall of 2003 the Villa's internal systems, including electrical, plumbing and heating, were replaced. Unfortunately for some, including Chope who liked to stay in his old bedroom occasionally but understood and supported the renovation, this meant the end of use for the Phillips family bedrooms. But since they were no longer used for guests they could now be part of Villa tours. The year 2004 saw repairs to the Villa's exterior tile work and courtyard fountains, and a new mini-pool for the gargoyle fountain on the edge of the old swimming pool. The roof was repaired beginning in 2005 and restoration of the doors and windows began in 2007.

Two other interesting Phillips possessions have also been recently repaired for the Villa museum. For many years a 1906 Ford Model "N" sat rusting in the garage at the Villa. Ranch committee member Chuck Walneck led an effort to restore the historic automobile and returned it to the ranch in September 2008. That fall a restoration of the Knabe grand player piano, a centerpiece of the Villa furnishings, began.

The Philmont Museum and Seton Memorial Library

Known as the Seton Memorial Museum and Library from its construction in 1967 to the name change in 1982 due to an expanding variety of collections, the Philmont Museum houses Southwestern art, area artifacts, Philmont history, historical literature of the Boy Scouts of America, and the extensive collection of Ernest Thompson Seton.

Seton (1860-1946) was one of the founders of the Boy Scouts of America, the BSA's first Chief Scout, and co-author with World Scouting's founder Robert Baden-Powell of the first BSA Handbook. A renowned artist and naturalist, he amassed an amazing collection of art, Native American and historical artifacts, books, and wildlife.

In 1965 his widow, Julia Seton, donated his entire collection to the Boy Scouts of America. In 1967 L. O. Crosby, Jr. provided the funding for the BSA to build a museum to house the collection at Philmont.

The museum's extensive collections are displayed on a rotating basis.

The Kit Carson Museum at Rayado

Most of the land that Waite Phillips gave to the Boy Scouts was the mountainous portion of his ranch which he thought would be best for a camping and hiking program. A major exception was the Southeast corner of the ranch and much of the Settlement of Rayado.

Rayado was established in the winter and spring of 1848 near a spot where the Taos Trail left the main Santa Fe Trail. One of the first settlers was Lucien Maxwell, the son-in-law of landowner Carlos Beaubien and friend of Kit Carson. Carson joined Maxwell in Rayado in 1849 and lived there off and on for about two years.

Nearly one-hundred years later, in 1941, Phillips asked the Scouts to rebuild Kit Carson's home and the other buildings at Rayado, including the Maxwell-Abreu home. Under the direction of a Taos contractor, and using plans provided by descendants of Maxwell, Scouts and Explorers staying at Rayado, or Carson-Maxwell as it was called in the early days of Philmont, made adobe bricks for the restoration of the Carson home. Several other buildings from the era were rebuilt by Philmont, and other new ones were built to support the Carson-Maxwell base camp and the training camps that were held at Rayado until 1993.

The Maxwell-Abreu home was used for many years as a seasonal and year-around residence. In the mid-1990s, under the direction of the National Park Service and other agencies, an architectural archaeology survey was done to determine the age of each portion of the home. This was a very invasive survey as walls and floors were opened to reveal the original Santa Fe Trail era structure and the age of subsequent additions. The cost of a full restoration has proven to be prohibitive and the home has remained vacant since the study.

The Chapel of the Holy Child across the street from the Maxwell home is maintained by Philmont but is owned by of the Catholic Diocese of Santa Fe. The chapel was built by Carlos Beaubien's daughter, Petra Beaubien Abreu, following the death of her husband Jesús in July 1900. The chapel is directly across the street from the front door of the Maxwell-Abreu home so that Mrs. Abreu could walk directly out her door to daily mass.

During the summer program months, the Rayado staff recreates life in a mid-19th Century Santa Fe Trail community with period costumes, furnishings, and activities.

CHAPTER TEN

The Campus

While the conference offerings and techniques may change, Scouters who come to the Training Center as youth, or come back after several years away, enjoy the "déjà vu" they feel as they drive past the cottonwood trees and up the road to PTC, as they move into their tent, or walk across the Greensward to the Villa Philmonte. The Training Center campus is not only a place for excellent training; it is a place of special Scouting and family memories. While there is obviously more to all that than just PTC's buildings, part of those experiences do come from the campus itself.

The Training Center began with a remodeled Villa kitchen and servants' quarters that could be used as a dining hall and meeting room, and a bunkhouse that was built "to house 96 men." As plans were being made for the future and the popularity of Philmont grew, it was quickly evident that a lot more of everything would be needed.

In late 1950, after just the first summer of national conferences, the Boy Scouts of America budgeted nearly half a million dollars for new facilities. By the summer of 1954 the Training Center boasted a new assembly hall and dining hall, a new conference building that could be divided into three rooms, duplexes for the conference faculty, and a new tent city. The basic configuration of today's PTC was in place.

Each part of the overall PTC campus and the related facilities has a bit of history of its own, and with only a few exceptions, were built with funds from the investment of Waite and Genevieve Phillips' endowment gifts. Their generosity continues in many, many ways.

PTC Office Complex

The first BSA building in the Villa area was today's PTC office complex. Originally built in 1942 as a bunkhouse for visitors to Philmont, the building had a small office on the south end, restrooms, and 10 sleeping rooms that would accommodate 96 men.

At times in the '40s and '50s two or more of the bunk rooms were converted to meeting rooms, but this drastically cut into the housing possibilities. In the '50s the north end was used as a nurse's station. The building was not used as the Training Center office until the mid-'50s when the small office was expanded to accommodate registration and the summer director. Prior to that expansion, the training center "office" was located in the East Tent City office and the director used space in the Villa's Trophy Room.

In 1968 the office was remodeled and expanded for the National Executive Institute staff.

The bunkhouse sleeping rooms remained in use for 50 summers (1942-1991) as housing for staff and single male faculty members. In 1992 the last sleeping rooms were converted into a conference room, a staff work room, and storage.

The first permanent conference room was converted from the nurse's station on the north end of the building. Originally called Rayado, this room was first used in 1957 and enlarged in 1992. In 1998 the room was renamed Carson to match the historical theme of the rest of the rooms, and to avoid confusion after the facilities at Rayado began to be used by the Training Center. Several individuals had driven the seven miles down to the site of the Settlement of Rayado community to find conferences when told they would be meeting in Rayado.

The second conference room was added in 1993 and was called Apache. In 1998 this room was renamed for George Webster. Webster was the rancher who owned much of the property, including the area around the Villa, which Phillips purchased to create his Philmont Ranch.

For many years the staff at Camping Headquarters moved into the Training Center office for the winter and this was the "off season" program office for the entire ranch.

In 2001-2002 the building underwent a major renovation.

East Tent City

East Tent City was the first tent city at PTC and was ready for the summer of 1951. The East Tent City office served as the "office" for thr training center for the first few years. The current tent city office was built in 1954 along with new shower/wash houses. The early shower houses were called service buildings and included washing machines, stoves, and refrigerators so that "mom could have all the comforts of home." The service buildings were remodeled in the mid-1980s.

Before the Handicraft Lodge was built, the East Tent City Office included a trading post and a craft area.

Assembly Hall

The Assembly Hall was part of the original 1950-approved construction project. In the early days each week consisted of one large, single-topic conference. As attendance increased, a large room that could handle all of the week's conference participants was needed to replace the relatively

The Assembly Hall, Dining Hall 1, and kitchen under construction in 1952. The buildings opened in time for the 1954 season.

small Villa conference/dining room. The ranch also had plans for square dances and other family activities that would provide the "Western fun" that Waite Phillips and Arthur Schuck envisioned.

The design of the Assembly Hall closely matched the original style of the Villa Philmonte, which ended at the Gazebo. Many Philmont visitors are not aware that it was an add-on by the BSA and think it was part of the original home.

The Assembly Hall has often been decorated with Scouting flags, paintings, and photos of Philmont. A mural of the Philmont mountains by Patty Taylor was on the wall behind the stage for many years. In 2008 a new mural of the mountains and the wildlife of the area was painted by Melinda Marlowe.

Dining Hall 1

Dining Hall 1 and the PTC kitchen were also part of the original expansion project that was completed in 1954. This addition greatly increased the capacity of the Training Center as conferences did not have to shut down and clear the Villa for meal preparation. This also took the burden of meal preparation away from the small Villa kitchen.

The dining hall was connected to the Assembly Hall with a partition for closing either facility off for concurrent use.

Like the Assembly Hall, the design of Dining Hall 1 matched the style of the Villa.

The dining hall kitchen was extensively remodeled and upgraded in 2006.

Dining Hall 2

Dining Hall 2 was built in 1957 with two serving lines. To aid in scheduling, and giving directions, the new dining hall was called Dining Hall 2 and Dining Hall 3 on the maps for many years. Participants came in the end doors and left out the center doors.

A heating system was added in 2001 so that Dining Hall 2 could be used year-around and PTC could host larger groups in the winter months.

Bent/Beaubien/Miranda

Originally built as part of the 1950-54 project, the original structure included only what is now the Bent and Beaubien classrooms. The building originally had three doors on the porch and accordion walls so that it could be separated into one, two, or three classrooms. This building gave the Training Center the facilities to host more than one conference at a time or to have break-out sessions for single conferences.

The building was remodeled and enlarged in 1968 when the National Executive Institute (NEI) was brought to Philmont to provide a western location for basic professional training. The original conference room was now divided by a solid wall with a smaller room named "Bent" in one-third of the space, and a larger "Beaubien" room in the other two-thirds. Another large classroom called "Miranda" was added, as well as restrooms, a porch, and an office for the NEI staff. The storage room was modified to provide media capabilities, including rear film projection into Beaubien and Miranda.

The old NEI office became the conference faculty office for many years, and in 2004 became the office of the Philmont Staff Association.

These rooms were named after important historical figures in Philmont country history: pioneers and landowners Guadalupe Miranda and Charles Beaubien, and New Mexico territorial governor Charles Bent.

Maxwell

Maxwell was added in 1965 as part of another Training Center expansion. Maxwell could be divided into two conference rooms with an accordion wall.

The room was named for pioneer landowner Lucien Maxwell.

South Tent City

Capacity at PTC was more than doubled with the addition of South Tent City in 1957. South Tent City matched the layout of East Tent City, with two shower houses and a tent city office.

Women participated in Cub Scouting conferences as early as 1952. These den mothers are working on puppets during a session in the old Bunkhouse. The old Bunkhouse is now the PTC office.

Laundry

The laundry building, which houses coin-operated washers and dryers for conference participants and a large laundry for the ranch operation, was built in the mid 1980s. Prior to this addition laundry facilities were located in each tent city service building and the Villa basement.

Bunkhouse

Originally built in 1957 as a Health Lodge, this building was later converted into a Nursery and family program office. The yard on the south side was fenced and had a playground. It remained a Nursery until 1994 when the new Small Fry Center opened. In 1994 and 1995 it was used as housing for cooks and senior dining hall staff. Beginning in 1996 it became housing for the PTC seasonal management staff.

Duplexes

The three duplexes on the greensward are the original duplexes built by the BSA for faculty housing in 1954. The others were built as part of ensuing expansions, with the last, and largest, built in 1999 in an area that used to be the PTC staff parking lot. Heating units were added in 1996 so that the duplexes could be used for conferences at any time of the year.

Multi-Plex

With the increased need for off-season roofed housing and an increasing number of conferences and faculty with families, the Multi-Plex was erected in 2003. The building was made possible by a gift from the estate of Allen Curtis.

Cottage

The Cottage is an original Phillips-era building, but was a kennel for the family dogs in those days. The BSA converted it into a residence in 1954 for summer visits by the BSA's Director of Phillips properties. Today it is used as housing for faculty and other guests of the ranch.

Philips Conference Rooms/Brown Building

In 1996 the Ranch Committee began the development of a long-range plan to address the needs of the Ranch's facilities for the new century. One of the needs was additional classroom space at PTC.

Unfortunately, two of the Training Center's seven classrooms were inadequate to meet the growing needs of conferences. One, Bent, was large enough to accommodate a conference of no more than 12 participants. The original Villa conference room was not handicapped accessible, had no restroom facilities, and was putting a strain on the aging Villa.

The committee determined that the construction of a new building that included a large, 100 person capacity, dividable conference room and storage facilities would meet the needs of the Training Center for the near future, and would allow for alternative uses for the existing rooms.

The family of Walter M. "Buster" Brown, III, a long-time Scouter and member of the Ranch Committee, decided that assisting the Ranch in building this facility would be a fitting tribute to the continuing dedication and devotion that Buster had to Scouting and Philmont, so they made a gift for a portion of the cost of the building.

In 1998 the building was completed and the twin classrooms were named after Waite (pronounced wait) Phillips and his twin brother Wiate (pronounced white), who died in Spokane, Washington when the boys were 18. Like Maxwell, and Beaubien/Bent before 1968, the rooms can be separated by a movable wall and can be made into one large classroom.

Villa Museum

The space occupied by the Villa Museum was originally servant's quarters for the Villa. In 1942 the space was converted into a dining room and classroom for the first training conferences at Philmont. With the addition of the 1954 dining hall, the room was used exclusively as a classroom until 1997. In 1998, the addition of the Phillips classrooms made it possible to again convert the room for use as part of the overall Villa museum.

Small Fry Center

The Small Fry Center was completed in 1994. It includes nap rooms, play rooms, restrooms, a kitchen, and attached playground for Philmont's youngest visitors. The funds to build the center were provided by a gift from the estate of prominent California livestock man Loren Charles Bamert.

Handicraft

In 1957 the current structure was built for "handicrafts, movies, and family parties" and was called the Recreation Building. The items carried at the Trading Post were limited by space and storage realities, so in 1996 the trading post was closed to give the craft operation more room. Another consideration in the decision to close the trading post was to encourage PTC families to go across the street to the camping headquarters trading post. Many families had left Philmont having not seen that part of the operation and the hundreds of Scouts arriving and departing each day. Ranch management wanted to expose at least part of the magnitude of the total operation to more participants. In 1998 there was another expansion creating an enlarged pottery and kiln area.

Rocky Mountain Scout Camp and Camp Urraca

After the summer of 1971 Camp Urraca, built in 1965 and located on the road to the Stockade at the present Badger Camp, was closed and replaced by Rocky Mountain Scout Camp. In 1992 the Boy Scout camping program was discontinued and moved back to PTC. The National Junior Leader Instructor Camp moved from Rayado to Rocky Mountain Scout Camp in 1994.

Many of the improvements in the facilities at Rocky Mountain Scout Camp were provided by two great Scouters: Jim Heath, and Scoutmaster of many National Junior Leader Instructor Camps Tom Krouskup.

Chapel

The PTC Chapel was built in 1959 by the Committee on Protestant Service of the Boy Scouts of America, chaired by Judge Charles W. Froessel of New York. Funds to build the chapel, and the chapel at camping headquarters that is now the Ranger Office, came from members of the committee and collections at Protestant services at the 1959 National Training Conference and the 1957 National Scout Jamboree. A dedication was held on August 2, 1959 during the Protestant Workshop on Scouting conference.

Project COPE Course

The Project C.O.P.E. (Challenging Outdoor Personal Experience) ropes and challenge course was built in part by a grant from the Order of the Arrow beginning in 1996. It was intended to be a model course with a wide variety of elements for training and local council review.

Hunting Lodge

The Hunting Lodge was one of Waite Phillips' mountain cabins. In the early years it was the site of the Cimarroncito Camp and where John Westfall wrote the words to the "Philmont Hymn" while a camper there in

1945. Concerns about the proximity of Cimarroncito's facilities to the source of the Village of Cimarron's drinking water supply convinced the Scouts to close the camp and move Cito to its present location farther up the meadow.

For many years the Lodge was used as a staff rendezvous. Various staff groups used the Lodge for staff celebrations and it fell into general disrepair. In 1994-1995 $50,000 was spent to restore the building and repair the sagging roof. There was no interest at the time in making it a new backcountry camp so the Training Center took it over. Furniture found in the building and other locations on the ranch was restored and the Lodge was put back in use. The Lodge was used as an overnight camping spot for the Muchachas program (11-13 year old girls), a day-hike destination for spouses, and outdoor skills training. It was the site of the first Venturing Powderhorn course in 1999. It was also often used by the Kanik winter camping program as a base.

In 1999 a historical program and tour at the Lodge was proposed for both Training Center participants and passing crews. Control of the Hunting Lodge was passed to the camping operation and the camp and a historical program was offered beginning in 2001.

Zastrow

In October 1948 the second Wood Badge training course in America had been conducted at Cimarroncito. For Philmont's second course in 1949, a new Wood Badge Lodge was built at the homestead site of early Colfax County settler, Paul F. Zastrow. The Lodge was remodeled in 1960.

The Wood Badge sundial at Zastrow was a gift from the Boy Scouts of England to the Boy Scouts of America in 1950. Its inscription says "Presented by the Scouts of the British Commonwealth and Empire in commemoration of forty years of Scouting by the Boy Scouts of America." The sundial was originally located at Schiff Scout reservation to recognize Schiff as the symbolic home of Wood Badge in the U.S. When the BSA closed Schiff in 1979, the sundial was moved to Zastrow to recognize it as the home of BSA Wood Badge.

Wood Badge courses were held at the site until 2002 when it became part of the backcountry mountain-biking program. The heritage of training and Wood Badge is part of the current camp program.

Rayado

One of the most historical – in terms of both New Mexico and Boy Scout history – places on the ranch, Rayado, started out as Rayado Rancho Base Camp and then Carson-Maxwell Base Camp. It was one of the main base camps for various camping and hiking expedition programs for many years. From 1946 to 1993 it was also the home of junior leader and Explorer training. Beginning in 1998, in an effort to expand conference offerings and provide a place for outdoor-oriented sessions, some conferences were held at the Rayado Dining Hall. The Dining Hall was also used as a location where Philmont could host special group meetings in the summer without interfering with conferences.

Program Bowl

The original PTC Program Bowl was located behind East Tent City to the north of the staff area, near where the warehouse and shop are today. In 1981 Philmont decided to build new program bowls for both PTC and Camping Headquarters and the PTC bowl was erected in its current location. The bowl was redesigned in 2007.

Stockade

The original Stockade was built in 1949 at a cost of $5,000. In 1960 it was destroyed by what was believed to be a tornado and was rebuilt at its current location at the base of the Tooth of Time. The Stockade has been used off and on by treks and the camping program at Philmont, including as the starting location for Kit Carson Treks and the ending location for Rayado Treks and Ranger training. For many years the site was used by the Cub Scout programs at PTC for day camp. After the Boy Scout program moved back to PTC in 1992, the Stockade was where a weekly Boy Scout overnight campout was held.

The original Stockade was built in 1949 for $5,000. It, and its replacement, have been used for a variety of programs – including a Cub Scout Day Camp and Boy Scout overnight camp.

Polo Barns

Polo was a popular sport among the ranchers of the area and Waite Phillips had one of the best facilities in the area. The barns included storage, stalls for horses, and homes for the wranglers. A polo field and track was located to the southeast of the barns.

The small fry center at the Polo Barns was opened in 1956. It was closed after the 1993 summer and moved to a new building near the PTC Handicraft Lodge.

In 1996 Philmont hired a food service company to prepare the meals at both Camping Headquarters and the Training Center. The old Polo Barns small fry center was renovated and turned into housing for their employees.

Pony Ring

The original pony ring was located where the PTC staff tent city is today, in the middle of an apple orchard. From 1956 to 1994 a pony ring was located at the Polo Barns. Photos of children riding the ponies with Tooth of Time Ridge in the background were often featured in magazines and promotional brochures.

In 1995 Ranch Superintendent Bob Ricklefs proposed building a new ring closer to the new Small Fry Center so that the youngsters would no longer need to be bused or have to cross the street to ride ponies. This also allowed parents to watch their children ride and children to be able to ride the ponies more often.

Shelters

Two shelters at PTC were built in 1997. The first, near the nature trail and the Ranch Administration area, was built with a fire pit to provide a location for Scouting skills training and a shelter for family program groups on the nature trail. The second, which was located at the north end of East Tent City and was sometimes called the Pavilion, was built to provide a shelter for faculty bar-b-ques and a rainy day location for family program groups.

In 2004 a new, much larger pavilion was erected for faculty bar-b-ques and the old pavilion was moved to the south end of East Tent City.

Urraca Trail

Many Scouters and families coming to PTC want to go on a hike. After all, that is what usually comes to mind when one thinks of Philmont. Many hiking opportunities were offered on the mid-week day off, including at times Zastrow, Hunting Lodge, Window Rock, Indian Writings, the T-Rex print, Lovers Leap, the Tooth of Time, and early on even Baldy.

Unfortunately, some of these hikes were and are beyond the physical capabilities of many participants, and large numbers of PTC day hikers were negatively impacting the remote wilderness experience of Scouts on backpacking treks.

In 1987 the Training Center designed and built a special trail just for PTC, in an area not used by treks. This trail presented wonderful views and a variety of vegetation zones, and included a guide map with markers to identify features. To make it even more attractive, a special patch was created for those who hiked the trail.

Over the years the trail has been expanded and rebuilt, most recently by the Philmont Staff Association.

CHAPTER ELEVEN

The Training Center In Scouting

One of the many attractions of the Training Center is that the more it changes the more it stays the same. A description of the Philmont Training Center geography, facilities, and program in any of several early 1950s Scouting magazines could probably be used today to promote PTC with only minor changes.

Over the years there have been some wonderful articles about the Training Center in the pages of *Scouting* magazine. *Scouting* was a key element in the promotion and early success of PTC and is an important factor today.

Since these articles give a snapshot of the early days, are often entertaining, and are pretty hard for most folks to find, a few of the early ones are included here.

May 1951 – (the first mention of the Training Center in Scouting*)*

Training at Philmont and Schiff

For volunteers who carry key responsibilities in Local Council administration, there are available two unique opportunities for training under the guidance of national leaders, and in an ideal setting.

These are definitely "plus" opportunities, unusual in their leadership, unusual in the calibre of men who attend, and unusual in their outdoor environment. They are designed for key men who can carry training back to the Local Council. In fellowship, in personnel, and in natural setting, they combine the best in training and the best in fun.

Now a series of courses at Philmont Scout Ranch combines the chance for top-flight training, with a chance to see this marvelous mountain country. Scouters all over the nation will want to avail themselves of this opportunity to visit the spot which has come to mean so much to a host of Explorers.

The first five conferences on the Philmont schedule – July 15 through August 25 – offer something new ... a vacation opportunity combined with some fine training. Scouters coming to these five conferences are invited to bring their wives; reservations should be made through the Local Council, and as far in advance as possible.

November 1951

Cub Scouters Pioneer at Philmont

During the summer of 1951 a total of 112 men, women and children participated in the first volunteer Cub Scouting Conference at the Philmont Boy Scout Ranch. These fine folks who came from 18 states and Mexico were pioneers in the true sense of the word since they represented Cub Scouting's first venture at the great mountain ranch.

National Cub Scout Committee Chairman John M. Bierer and National Committeeman R. E. Eckles were on hand to mark this first step by the Boy Scouts of America in conducting combination vacation and Cub Scouting adventure for entire families. The ages ran from two up to one Cubmaster who surely was the granddad of all Cubmasters in the land. The families lived in a glorified tent city, the tents having spring cots, wooden floors – even private small tents for the children.

The conference was not only a work session but a great family venture. Thirty-five men, women and children went on a long horseback expedition to the Tooth of Time. There was a special day set aside for long expeditions. Everyone went off to see such spots as the Pueblo Indian village at Taos and the beautiful city of Santa Fe. There were bus and motor caravan trips across the entire Philmont mountain range.

In addition to the conference sessions and family recreation periods there was a complete program for children. The activities included popular nature hunts which uncovered hundreds of nature objects including several horned toads. There were special craft periods, story hours, fun nights, puppet plays, horseshoe tournaments and game hours.

The business side of the conference included open forum discussions on all subjects which the group wanted to discuss; an evening games session based upon the Pow Wow Games Section; interesting projects in connection with basic training, and special exhibits and demonstrations provided by the members of the conference. Informal discussion carried on in the big house until the wee small hours.

In the near future *Scouting* Magazine will give information about plans for the second National Conference of Cub Scout leaders, to be held at Philmont in 1952. It is hoped that this will be the greatest gathering of Cub Scout leaders ever to take place in America.

December 1951

Family Vacation and Scouter Training at Philmont

Already Scout families all over America are thinking of next summer's trip to Philmont Scout Ranch at Cimarron, New Mexico. They think of it as their ranch – this 127,000 acre stretch of land in N.E. New Mexico. You too, may come to Philmont for training and a grand vacation.

The Training Conferences provide instruction by nationally known instructors who will teach you how to use your time and energy most effectively in giving leadership to the Scout program.

During your stay at Philmont there will be opportunities for you to see the great Scout Ranch in operation and to visit its outstanding scenic and historic spots – Ponil, Cimarroncito, Kit Carson's home and the beautiful Abreu country. The mountains, wooded valleys, plateaus and fertile plains abound with wild game and the streams are filled with gamy fish. Those who have visited Philmont are high in the praise of its beauty.

Today you can still see the deep ruts left by the wagon trains on the old Santa Fe Trail which traversed the area now known as Philmont. The robust days of the Old West are frequently brought to mind around the campfires which take place on the very spot where pioneers pitched their tents or stopped their prairie schooners.

The new Assembly Hall gave PTC a large facility that could accomodate much larger conferences and events. Assistant Director of Cub Scouting Marlin Sieg leads a session during a mid-1950s conference.

Yes sir, bring your family. Facilities are now available to accommodate families of Scouters who are participating in Conferences and Training events on the Ranch. Special programs will be offered for family groups – nature hikes, games and general sight-seeing trips. Social gatherings and rainy day programs in the Big House will also be scheduled.

A comfortable "tent city" provides roomy space for family groups. Housekeeping duties are reduced to a minimum. Even large family groups will find facilities for every need. Tents are provided with a wooden floor and comfortable beds.

January 1952

National Conference of Cub Scout Leaders

August 3rd-9th, 1952, will be one of the most important weeks in the Cub Scouting calendar. That week will mark the opening of the National Conference of Cub Scout Leaders at Philmont Scout Ranch, Cimarron, New Mexico. It will be the greatest national gathering of Cub Scout Leaders in the history of our Movement.

Not only will it be the richest Cub Scouting experience ever offered, but it will also provide Cub Scout Leaders and their families one of the finest vacation experiences of their lives. The conference schedule will leave plenty of time for fishing, hiking, some horseback riding, and sightseeing in the historic Southwest country. The mountains, trout streams, wildlife and real western ranching operations are only a few of the things which make Philmont an attractive vacation land.

There will be an opportunity to build Cub Scouting friendships with people from all corners of America. It will be Cub Scouting's greatest trading spree, because everyone will be loaded with gadgets and ideas to swap.

The conference program will be packed with new "how" material, and will be organized on the university plan. Certain major subjects will be offered in the morning, each person choosing one such major. The major subjects will run throughout most of the conference.

On certain afternoons minor subjects will be offered, each person choosing two. These subjects will be of shorter duration, and there will be a wide variety from which to choose.

Major subjects will include theme crafts, game leadership, puppetry and dramatics, Pack administration, the knack of leadership, etc. Minor subjects will include song leading, ceremonies, story telling and play acting, tricks and puzzles, Den meeting programs, Indian lore, etc.

The conference evenings will be devoted to social activities and features which will finish off each day with a refreshingly different experience.

The various subjects presented at the conference will be led by outstanding authorities. Members of the staff of the National Cub Scouting Service and members of the National Committee on Cub Scouting will also give leadership to many of the conference activities. Leaders will receive the best in every subject included in the program.

During the last portion of the conference an entirely new approach will be made. At this point the entire conference will change from learning and getting, to giving and building. Each leader will be assigned to a specific project which will be undertaken as his obligation to the Scouting Movement. Thus the entire conference will devote itself to the creation of new Cub Scouting ideas and materials which will in turn find their way into the program during the year ahead.

Special activities will be offered for children. These activities will be under competent supervision and will make it possible for both mothers and dads to participate in the conference sessions. There will also be recreational programs for family groups.

Facilities at Philmont are being greatly enlarged for the 1952 conference, so leaders may bring their families with them. Those wives who are interested in Cub Scouting may join in the conference sessions. The fee will be $5 per day for each man and woman. This includes both meals and lodging. For those taking the training an additional $5 fee will be charged to cover training materials.

The rates for children are as follows: Daughters over 14 – $5 per day. (It is expected that sons 14 years of age or over will register for some Philmont camping schedule going on in the same period.) Children 5-13 years of age – $2.50 per day. Children through 4 years of age – $1 per day. It should be obvious to everyone that these fees are far below the normal fees for most vacation experiences.

Facilities are necessarily limited and will have to be allotted on a first come-first served basis. If you are interested in participating in this greatest of all Cub Scout experiences get in touch with your Local Council immediately, in order that they may take steps to request space for you.

January 1952

Tell 'Em You'll Be There

Philmont – the gathering place of famous Explorers – again invites you and your family to take part in the now popular family conferences.

These conferences are where you and other Explorer leaders get leadership training with time out for vacation – and where the wives and children just vacation.

Tell us that you'll be there at one of the Explorer conferences at Philmont Scout Ranch.

Yes, tell us you'll be there. One of the high spots of your family's experience will be your trip to Philmont.

- Walking along the trail with your partner, facing the future together as did your pioneer ancestors.
- Living in the land of enchantment where you can almost reach out and touch the stars.
- Meeting new leaders and their families from all parts of America.
- Seeing Philmont in action – watching boys become men in God's great out-of-doors.

Plenty of time to spend with the little lady every afternoon and plenty of time for her to be on her own with the other gals – swappin' recipes and having a corkin' good time.

A program for all children through thirteen years of age will be provided. Boys fourteen and over will be expected to register with one of the Philmont Schedules going on at the same time.

The conference in which you will play a most important part will be a real National Conference with an exchange of ideas and working methods dealing with how to help that teen-ager.

February 1953

Leadership At Two National Training Centers

The Volunteer Training Center at Philmont Scout Ranch will again offer Volunteer Scouters across America the vacation opportunity of a lifetime. And training, too!

Here's the story. Any Scouter may register for one of the conferences and bring his family along. In 1952, 777 men availed themselves of this opportunity, and most of them brought their families!

The dates are vacation-tailored. Each conference starts with the noon meal on Wednesday and ends with breakfast on the following Tuesday. This schedule fits perfectly into a two-week period which begins and ends on a week-end.

Special provision is made for the recreational needs of children 7-13 years of age. A fine supervised playground, pony riding, craft program, hikes and trips will keep them happy and busy. For the small fry (children 6 and under), a nursery program takes them at 9 A.M. and brings them back at 4 P.M. fed, napped and happy. Mom has at least seven hours when she may pursue her own pleasure.

The Tent City got rave notices from men and women alike. Innerspring beds, electric lights, floors, chairs and other items and equipment make the oversize tent as comfortable a dwelling as could be had. The kids love this "camping out" and even the ladies who were tenting for the first time found the experience great fun.

In each half of Tent City the shower house facilities are very complete. Imagine – a laundry room with automatic washer, and kitchen with stove and icebox for preparing baby formula or storing it.

Meals are served cafeteria style and the pattern of excellence has already been established in this phase of Philmont living. You just can't eat any better anywhere in the Southwest than you can at the Training Center.

The program offers many opportunities for hours of pleasure. Breathtaking, beautiful scenery surrounds the Center. Tours, horseback riding and free-time wandering will let you get acquainted with the whole Ranch. Crafts, games and just plain lounging will let you see it from your tent home. Take your choice! The program is flexible, in order that you may see and do the things you want most.

The Conference schedules are so established that Dad, Mother and the youngsters will have plenty of time together. Good roads go to the Ponil, Carson Maxwell and Cimarroncito Base Camps. Taos Indian pueblo is only 65 miles away. Fishing spots are close at hand. Truly, this is a vacation wonderland, and with flavor of Scouting fellowship added for good measure.

April 1953

Like a Vacation?

Philmont is an ideal vacation land, and it's all yours! Its trout filled streams, its breathtaking scenery, its cool and grassy mountain meadows are waiting for you this summer. Famous Philmont training awaits you too. There will be conferences for Finance committee members,

Commissioners and District and Council operating committees.

The Finance conference includes among the subject matter Local Council Finance planning, Council campaign techniques, community campaigns, trust fund promotion techniques and community chest relationships. Dates are July 8-15.

The District Operations conference is being held for the first time at the Training Center. The conference is pointed at all District personnel, except Finance chairmen and Commissioners. Dates are July 29 – August 4, 1953.

The Commissioners' conference will be based on the job of the Commissioner with these two general job descriptions:

1. District Commissioner – To recruit, train and supervise an adequate staff of Neighborhood Commissioners: 2. Neighborhood Commissioner – To keep his Units alive and healthy. Dates are July 1-7; July 15-21; July 22-28.

While dad participates in the Training Conference with other Scouters from all over the country, Mom and the children can have the time of their lives!

"Kit Carson slept here." Only fifteen minutes from the Training Center Tent City is Kit Carson's home. Along the roadside to Carson-Maxwell Base Camp the deep ruts cut by the covered wagons of early settlers and traders still crease the soil.

The "small fry" are taken over and given care, fed lunch, given a rest period and kept occupied all day. They're even taken on a picnic in the hills once during the week.

The older children, 6-14, are given an organized program throughout the week. Games, hikes, riding and craft work are all available.

The gracious rooms of the Villa Philmonte are open for reading, good talk or just lounging. Shady lawns invite relaxation, and the many miles of good roads on the ranch invite casual sight-seeing. The whole ranch is a photographer's and naturalist's paradise.

In addition, Mom will find so many home conveniences that taking care of the family will be easy. The over-sized tents have inner-spring beds, clothes closet, table, chairs, electric light, and all linens furnished. Automatic washing machines, refrigerators and stoves are available. All of the comforts of home – but no cooking to do, no dishes to wash!

You're invited. Ask your Scout Executive for folders describing the Conference you want to attend. He'll give you a reservation blank, too. Start the ball rolling toward the vacation of a lifetime! NOW!

October 1953

Scouters Have Fun Too!

Dear Doc, (Harold West, the National Director of the Exploring Service)

You asked that we write to tell you the most important thing we got out of our stay at Philmont. The wheels of our little convertible had rolled nearly three thousand miles homeward before I could "see the forest for the trees." The "trees" were beautiful and I loved them. There were the stately pines of peaceful hours, the great oaks of friendship, aspens shaking with the excitement of new adventure, and cotton woods covering everything with the white happiness of all us being together at Philmont.

But to answer your question – from Philmont I brought a feeling of great respect.

Respect for the men from all walks of life who so unselfishly give not their wealth but themselves that the boys of America may have the benefits, skills and ideals of Scouting. There at Philmont I saw those volunteer Scouters from all over the country, from all walks of life, from all professions, hard working men who were willing to give their few hours of leisure to the boys of their home town – some of the towns little crossroads on the map, some of them dirty mining towns, some of them vast cities, but in all of these towns boys in need of men to lead them.

Respect for the professional Scouter; his ability to deal wisely and kindly with all the various personalities that make up the vast army of volunteer workers, to inspire and direct them. All of you have a remarkable executive ability, coupled with a willingness to attend to minute details – not often associated with the executive type.

Respect for the Scouts I saw in Philmont. All of them seemed to have taken on some of the dignity of the vast country of New Mexico. Many, facing new adventures alone, had quite serious misgivings but all of them – my son included – came out of the hills considerably farther along the road to manhood.

Respect for God. I'm so glad that you opened the gates of Philmont to Him. He walked so naturally among us in the foothills of the Sangre de Christo Mountains. Beneath the stars that seemed so close, men spoke His words so simply in the different accents of the various sections of the country. Surely "out in God's country" we all felt a deeper feeling of respect for our Maker. "I have seen Him in the campfires...."

There are those who say the professional Scouter has an easy life. Sometimes we call the Scout leader a sucker. There are those who scoff at the Boy Scouts and call them "sissies." But at Philmont, where the air is so clear, I saw them all with a keener vision and a wider perspective, and to them all I give my deep and sincere respect.

April 1954

It Pays to Go West

If you've been fighting down the urge to follow Horace Greeley's advice to "Go West" – just relax. Now is the time to go! It's never been easier to go west and never has it been more fun or less expensive.

The Volunteer Training Center at Philmont Scout Ranch is a ready-made terminus for your trip to the land of the ten-gallon hat, the war bonnet and "Howdy, Pardner."

The conference leaders are nationally known Scouters. The instruction includes the very latest in information and the finest in techniques.

Here's what a Scouter had to say about his family's 1953 stay at the Training Center. "The fellowship of other Scouters during those six days was an inspiration that will stay with me for the rest of my years. During our entire stay my wife, my children and I were comfortable and happy. The family camp arrangement gave us more fun at a low cost than we have ever had. We all want to go back again."

"The Training Center and program were excellent! It's too bad all leaders can't share in this experience."

"Wife enjoyed it very much, wanted to stay another week."

"I do not believe you can improve the women's and children's programs. They were almost perfect."

One had this to say about their stay: "Believe the personnel, program, materials and facilities were 'tops.' Many thanks for one of life's finest experiences."

Over 2300 men, women, and children came to the Training Center in 1953. They had a good time. They liked the food and found the accommodations pleasant and comfortable.

Another sums it all up very well. "The hustle-bustle of sleeping, eating, Conference, square dances, movies, handicraft, general good living and the clean associations of a group representative of America ..... clean thoughts, clean people – Philmont."

January 1955

Mom Goes to Philmont

(The comments from "Mom" that make up the majority of this article were accompanied by photos of family activities.)

Howdy! I'm Willard from Anthony, Kansas. For some time we'd talked about taking one of those family vacations at Philmont, the big Scout ranch near Cimarron, New Mexico. While I was taking my course at the training center there, Mom and the kids would be enjoying a real western vacation. Well, last summer we finally did it. It took some selling to get mom there, and when we arrived she – but I'll let her tell what happened. Mom take over!

Well, here we are! It'll be fine for Will with his training course, and the kids'll love it here. But guess who's going to be the official baby sitter? Me!

I must say the food here is certainly delicious! This would be an ideal vacation if I didn't have to watch the youngsters all week.

Say! Maybe I won't after all. It seems they have a supervised recreational program for the children here. That's our Dana on the lead pony there, folks.

And here are Mike and Pat going full tilt in the handicraft shop here. You can make almost anything you want. Expert instruction, too.

Here are the boys on an afternoon hike. Supervised activities like these happen every day here. And where are the mothers – ?

We mothers – glory be! – are Scot free to get together and plan our own activities. Here's our program committee getting some expert help in planning.

And here's one of the things we planned – a real western square dance! The kids? They're on hand tonight, too. Philmont's a "whole family" place.

Horseback riding is tops at Philmont. Here we are getting ready to head out for an exciting ride into the hills. Planned it ourselves, too.

Heavens! I almost forgot about Will, back in his training course. He met a wonderful group of men there, he tells me, and learned a lot.

Time to go home already? Good gracious, how did this wonderful week go by so fast? That's us there, in front to that fabulous Philmont scenery.

Will says he's not sure yet where we'll go on vacation next summer! Can you keep a secret? I've already made up his mind – PHILMONT!

What about your '55 vacation – Considered Philmont?

May-June 1955

Our Family Enjoyed Philmont

Gentlemen:

To say "thank you" seems so few words to express an appreciation. However, from Lewis, Thelma, and Robert comes a great big "thank you." While we were at Philmont we enjoyed ourselves very, very much. In fact, I have a confession. When Lew, my husband mentioned to Bob and me that he would like to go to Philmont last summer as part of his vacation we both had doubts – lots of them – about the value of the entertainment we would get out of it. Had we known more about Philmont our fears would have been calmed immediately because we had the time of our lives there. Now we are talking about how soon we can get back to Philmont. Here is just a part of what we have to say about our week there:

FROM LEW: I enjoyed my time at Philmont. "Doc" West and his staff made the week a complete one. The training and field experience we received while there was a most complete education in the Explorer way of life and program. I am more enthusiastic than ever before about getting an Explorer group together and serving as their leader. I hope also that when this has been accomplished the whole unit can go to Philmont. The movies which we took at Philmont will sell the idea.

FROM THELMA: I have from the earliest part of my life always feared horses. It was at Philmont I learned not only to trust these animals but to really love them. I only hope that when we get back to Philmont I might be able to spend more time horseback riding. At the same time I must also compliment your group at the Hobby Shop for the most enjoyable and educational training I received there. The setup in general for the family, the children's programs, the leaders' programs, the laundry situation, the tent arrangement, and not to be overlooked, the food situation! To mention them in the order which I have seems just like a lot of words but I just can't seem to express exactly my appreciation for all the enjoyment I received out of this.

FROM BOB: Boy, oh boy, did I have the best time of my life on my vacation! I had more fun riding the horses. I found out just how big and grown-up I can be and am when I am on a horse. I hope to spend more time riding the horses when I get back there. I had lots of fun learning about different things in the Hobby Shop. The movies were lots of fun and I enjoyed my tent life too. Altogether, I want to go back again and soon.

FROM ALL OF US: Our thanks to all of you who had a share in making our stay at Philmont so enjoyable that we are looking forward to going back there. Your kitchen staff is not to be overlooked either. The food was so good we were afraid of staying there any longer for fear of the overstuffed look we would have when we got home. Thanks again, and we are really looking forward to seeing you in the very near future.

We Found Scouting's Heart

How would you like to go to Philmont Scout Ranch in New Mexico for our vacation next summer?" asked my husband, one snowy February evening when he came home from a neighborhood Scout workers' meeting.

"Philmont!" our children breathed reverently, their nostrils already dilating with mountain air.

"Don't be silly!" I answered. "I can't shoulder a pack. I can't march off into the wild blue yonder mountains. I can't . . ."

"You don't do any of those things at the volunteer training center," he interrupted. "Sure, we'll live in tents, but everything else is solid comfort. Just you wait and see!"

I never quite believed his extravagant picture of Philmont, but nevertheless I became infected with the family's enthusiasm as vacation time arrived.

With mounting excitement, we approached New Mexico from southeastern Colorado over breath-taking Raton Pass into New Mexico. Its sweeping panorama of great distances and majestic Sangre de Cristo Mountains made New Mexico's slogan, "Land of Enchantment," understandable.

Though we wanted to linger, the thrill of being so near Philmont spurred us on, over Highway 64, to Cimarron, where we turned south to Philmont.

"Buffalo! Antelope!" our children shouted, and they all four leaned out one side of the car as we passed a securely fenced in area.

Arriving at Tent City, with its row of high-flying, bright flags, the children could restrain themselves no longer. Susan, eight, and Danny, five, headed for the playground where swings, merry-go-rounds, and teeter-totters were already swarming with other youngsters. Tom, eleven, and Jim, thirteen, were immediately involved in a volleyball game with other boys their age.

"Well," grinned Dad, "I said you wouldn't have to shoulder a pack, but you may have to help carry the suitcases to our tents, unless you can break up those games."

"Not bad," I had to admit, as we peeked in the tents. Our family got three wood-floored tents, each with two single beds, complete with sheets and wool blankets. "A closet—and an electric light! Even two lawn chairs— so far so good. Now I wonder where I wash all our dirty clothes? In some babbling brook?"

The solution turned out to be an automatic washer in the nearby service building, where rest rooms and showers were located. "Hi! My load of clothes will be done in five minutes if you want the machine," a friendly gal from Salt Lake City greeted me.

"I'm almost ready to concede," I told my husband, "that we won't have to eat our meals around a campfire."

"Soft lights and sweet music, just like I promised you," he answered as we walked up to the Big House. This had been the palatial Spanish-style residence of Waite Phillips, oil millionaire and donor of Philmont. At one end, a large dining room built in matching style accommodated dozens of tables. A huge lounge room, with comfy sofas, was dominated at one end by bigger-than-life paintings of a Cub Scout, a Boy Scout, and an Explorer. Strains of the "Grand Canyon Suite" filtered from one corner.

That did it! "Do you suppose they'll let us come back again next year?" I asked. "This is paradise."

"Scout-style paradise," my husband amended.

"Want to see the blood brother of the original head that the buffalo nickel was drawn from?" someone asked. "It's downstairs in the trophy room." So our children raced down to the collection of stuffed native animals and patted a huge buffalo head over the fireplace.

Next we visited the trading post, where we purchased souvenirs, Indian jewelry, and cards. Then we peeked at the small, but complete infirmary. It was comforting to know that medical care was available and free, if anyone needed it.

At a Scout official's invitation, many of us decided to take a tour of the surrounding plateau and mountains.

Before the construction of additional conference rooms, breakouts were held wherever space allowed, as was the case with this Cub Scouting conference breakout in the Villa's Gazebo in the early 50s.

During the trip we learned that Philmont has three separate, cooperating parts. One is the Volunteer Training Center for families, our Tent City.

Another is the ranching operation, for Philmont has a self-supporting ranch as a part of the 127,000 acres. In addition to the ranch herds, one can find, among the craggy mountains, elk, bear, bobcat, mountain lion, wild turkey, beaver, deer, antelope, and an infinite variety of birds. Plus jack rabbits unlimited! This sounded like paradise to city-bred boys. However, our only liaison with these animals was a family of bunnies who lived under the floor of the boys' tent.

The third part of Philmont, perhaps the soul of it, belongs exclusively to Explorers, Scouts who are fourteen years or over. They have three base camps, where each summer 10,000 boys come for an "expedition" of twelve days, or to participate in a junior leader training course. They hike or combine hiking with burros along to carry packs. Each boy also has the opportunity of riding horseback during his stay. They are given thorough physical checkups, for the trips are rugged, though not dangerous. Occasionally, in the days ahead, as we drove around the ranch we'd see these boys plodding along, or see their pin points of campfires at night.

110

Our guide took us to the reconstructed adobe house that had been Kit Carson's, for years ago part of the ranch had been his land, and the road we were following was once the glamorous Santa Fe Trail, life line of the Old West. Part of Carson's ancient home is used as a museum.

That evening, after a dinner of roast beef, mashed potatoes, asparagus, salad, and strawberry shortcake, everyone met in the big activity room for plan making.

It all boiled down to this: while Dad gets a thorough, inspirational Scout workshop, Mother gets a vacation, free from housework, cooking, and child care. And the children get a taste of ranch life in doses suited to their ages.

"Guess what, Mom?" said Danny. "Every morning I'll go in a school bus to a special spot on the ranch. We'll play games and have lunch there. We won't come back till almost supper time. And our bus driver says we sing songs all the time we're on the bus. He's going to teach us cowboy songs."

"I'll be a Kit Carson girl," said Susan, "and we'll meet every morning for games, handicraft, and songs. There are a dozen ponies out in the corral, and we get to ride them. Your group does too, Danny."

"We're in the Kit Carson boys' group," said Tom. "That's for boys seven to fourteen years old. We'll have volleyball, baseball, and mountain fishing. And handicraft if we want it."

"Just think," said Jim, eyeing the distant mountain trails wistfully, "if I were only a few months older, and fourteen already, I could go out tonight on a five-day camping trip. Wouldn't that be cool!"

The meeting ended with a song festival, topped off by the deeply moving Philmont hymn. We all headed for our tents. Those of us who were novices to mountain temperatures were amazed by the chill night air, for the day had been hot. Our altitude, over 6,000 feet, caused this and we soon adjusted to it. Although it was cold at night, the heat was back early each morning, teasing us from our mountain of covers.

The world's largest remuda of saddle horses awaits Philmont riders, so the next day forty of us tried some out, riding up a steep mountain trail for a splendid panorama of the Big House and Tent City, against a backdrop of the Philmont plateau and the rugged Sangre de Cristo mountains.

That evening there was a square dance, and our husbands, who had been busy all day in training course activities, joined us in the fun.

The next few days slipped by in a delightfully lazy pattern of leisure, handicraft, and forays into the countryside for us wives, and a variety of exciting activities for the children.

On Sunday we were free to take trips on our own. Our family chose Taos and Santa Fe, both richly Spanish in architecture and atmosphere, and both steeped in the romantic history of the colorful early West.

Back at Philmont that night, every family was excited about its day's travels. Some had gone to Raton to swim, others to Cimarron. Some groups had visited Scout base camps, others had taken the scenic Red River Canyon drive. Everyone was anxious to tell of his trip, but a turkey dinner got top attention.

"Only one more day at Philmont" was the sorry realization on Monday morning. Though we were all to leave Tuesday morning, somehow we'd been hoping it would go on indefinitely. Everyone tried to cram as much fun, handicraft, sun-tanning, and horseback riding as possible into the final day. After dinner, skits and songs added to the festive, though nostalgic, atmosphere.

Although no dance was scheduled, everyone demanded – and got – one. So we had a last late night of fun. Like one big congenial family, everyone seemed reluctant to break Scout ties and scatter to the four winds.

It had been a week of incomparable fellowship, and best of all, because it's the real reason for this Tent City, a week of intensive training that would spell better Scouting in every community represented.

What does Philmont, deep in the "Land of Enchantment," do to your heart to cause the deep devotion we all felt? On our last evening there I listened to the Philmont hymn, ringing out over the cool night air into the mysterious mountains and let the words etch themselves into my heart.

Silver on the sage, starlit skies above,
Aspen-covered hills, country that I love.
Philmont here's to thee,

Scouting paradise,
Out in God's country tonight.

Wind in whispering pines,
Eagles soaring high,
Purple mountains rise against an azure sky.
Philmont, here's to thee,
Scouting paradise,
Out in God's country tonight.

Then I looked around the room, dominated at one end by the three enormous lighted pictures, a Cub Scout, a Boy Scout, and an Explorer. I watched the happy family groups, expressing the best in American living and the highest in Scout ideals. Tomorrow it would all end. Or would it? For, as a result of this experience, we would all be better individuals, better families, better Scouters. I'm sure each heart echoed my thought:

Philmont—someday we'll be back again!

February 1962

Hey Wives! Be Queen for a Week

What about this place called Philmont? We'd heard a lot about it, including the possibility for a fine family vacation. Well, that would remain to be seen.

It was novel for the entire family to be included in a Scouting expedition. Oh, we'd had our share of cooking for Scout dinners, providing transportation for campouts, hauling bundles for paper drives, and turning out en masse to see our Boy Scout receive his hard-earned awards. But, in all of these activities we were more of less in the role of spectators. Halfway expecting the same thing at Philmont, I was pleasantly surprised.

Scouting is primarily a "stag" affair. But Scouts have mothers . . . and sisters . . . and little brothers. And fortunately (or unfortunately as the case may be) Scout leaders have wives.

Many a promising leader has been lost to Scouting because his wife was jealous of the days and nights he spent working with boys. And show me a Scouter's wife who hasn't sat out a business-as-usual vacation at home while her volunteer leader took his precious accumulated vacation time to go camping with the Scouts.

We women know a good supporting Scout wife is worth her weight in merit badges. The question is "Does the National Council know it, too?" The answer is: "Yes."

Philmont is a place where the family is "included in." A place where wives and sons and daughters can enjoy a vacation while the volunteer leader soaks up a headful of Scouting instruction.

What's in it for us "girls" at Philmont? First of all, the biggest burden – that of child-tending – is taken from the wife's shoulders for the six days she is there. Philmont has a planned program for all age groups from diapers to high heels. Activities begin at 9 A.M. and continue through to 4:30 P.M. each day except Sunday. The small fry, ages six and under, board a bus for the Small Fry Center down the canyon, where they are entertained, fed, and well cared for during the day.

Cub Scout age boys, Kit Carson Girls, and Kit Carson Boys (up to thirteen) also have their planned activities that include hikes, picnics, tours, contests, and pony riding. Boys over fourteen can spend the week camping in the canyon.

Second, the wife's housekeeping burdens are at a minimum. Meals are served cafeteria style in the dining halls. If, however, she has an uncontrollable domestic urge, she can swish a broom through her tent or run a load of washing through an automatic washer or brew a pot of coffee in the kitchen-laundry nearest her tent.

Aside from these strenuous housekeeping chores, the great attraction is Villa Philmonte, the beautiful ranch home built by Mr. and Mrs. Waite Phillips and donated with furnishings intact at the time Philmont's 127,000 acres were given to the Boy Scouts of America. The house is open to tours and the game room is a haven for the inevitable bridge sharks who find their way to Philmont.

If bridge isn't her game, there are many other activities for the Scouting wife. She can make a tour to the Kit Carson Museum, which is staffed (as is the entire camp) by delightful Explorer-age boys, who really get a charge out of showing off the museum's treasures with appropriate explanations.

The artists have plenty to sketch; the photographers have many pictorial treasurers to preserve. There are handicrafts for the handy, nature hikes and horseback riding for the outdoor lovers; historical tours for the history lovers; or just plain woman-type gab fests, which, of course, are the most fun of all.

The evenings are always busy with family programs, shows, or dances. On Sunday, following church services, the family can take a picnic lunch to one of the beautiful canyons within the ranch area or visit the Indian writings and diggings at Ponil.

It seems the most enjoyable times were spent just talking. Talking to people while standing in line at the cafeteria in the laundry at the trading posts or in the tent city. Lots and lots of friendly people from all over the United States.

One family with seven children traveled last summer from Massachusetts to New Mexico, camping along the route both ways.

Boss Sanchez, Philmont horse foreman from 1937 to 1983, leads a family ride from the Camping Headquarters corral in the early 50s.

Another family of five, with the mother in a wheelchair, spent an enjoyable week at the Training Center. With the aid of a devoted husband and some friendly neighbors, the wife missed out on none of the activities.

When you find people of like interests traveling from more than forty states to Philmont, you also find pleasure and good fellowship. Like the others before us, we fell in love with Philmont.

Philmont has charm. Its climate is excellent. It has beauty and vastness, but these are only contributing factors. I found the real secret of Philmont's charm in our last hours there. We were among the last to leave our conference. As each family pulled away, with fond farewells, Philmont lost a corresponding amount of its charm, until, at last, it was only a hollow shell. A lovely shell, to be sure, but still devoid of the vibrant life it had possessed during the week. Philmont's charm is in the people that go there.

January 1965

Philmont Honeymoon

The other day I surprised my husband by remarking that I was looking forward to visiting Philmont Scout Ranch again. He told me that until now he never quite knew if I had enjoyed the ranch. Of course I did. Our trip to New Mexico two years ago was more than a vacation. It was a wonderful honeymoon.

I thought that Les was kidding when he first suggested that we go to Philmont after the wedding. I had seen the pictures of his previous treks on the ranch trails and couldn't imagine myself hiking with a packsack or sleeping on the ground.

But there was another side to Philmont, he explained. This was the Volunteer Training Center for Scouters and their entire families.

We arrived at the ranch after a pleasant auto trip, sprinkled with sightseeing. All of Philmont's training courses start on Wednesday and terminate on the following Tuesday. This affords plenty of traveling time to and from the ranch.

Our accommodations were not Waldorf but wall tent. Tent city was spacious and comfortable, every tent having a wood floor, two beds, warm blankets, a small wardrobe closet, a table and chairs, and electricity. It was just a short walk from our tent to the laundry house with its automatic washers. Adjoining this building were the washrooms equipped with showers.

We had our meals at one of the beautiful dining halls. The other women at the training center welcomed the holiday from kitchen chores, but, being a newlywed, I did not fully understand the happiness. I do now.

What really impressed me at Philmont was the fact that there was something for everyone from the smallest tots to the teen-agers. Even the teen-age girls who were sure they would be overlooked at a boys' ranch were sorry to see their Philmont vacation end. One evening there was a dance for the teen-agers – after the adults were shooed to bed.

While the men attended their classes, we wives had the run of the ranch. We went on conducted tours of Philmont camps and interesting nearby sights of New Mexico, played cards, took lessons in handicraft, haunted the Western antique shops in Cimarron, or just lapped up the luxury of the Villa Philmonte, the beautiful mansion that Waite Phillips gave to the Boy Scouts of America.

There was plenty of free time for family events such as horseback riding or visiting a tourist site. Les and I ventured to Taos for a glimpse of the Indian pueblo dwellings and Kit Carson's home.

We have so many things to recall: the evening the buffalo herd came out of their pasture and into camera range, the buffalo roast that was quite a tasty treat, the wonderful campfire programs under the vast southwestern sky, and the gay Saturday night square dance.

Most of all I'll remember the wonderful people we met at Philmont. There was the mother who proudly wore her home-district "Scout Widow" name tag and the couple who brought their family of 11 kids along. I learned that Scouting is one tremendously big, happy family.

The wife of a 50-year Scouter gave me some sound advice. "If you want to keep your new husband happy," she said, "let him Boy Scout."

Did I enjoy Philmont? You bet I did. And I know I'll enjoy our second Philmont honeymoon as much as I did our first.

Afterword

The first time I ever heard the word Philmont was in 1971 when my father announced that we would be going there for our summer vacation. He had been invited to attend a commissioner conference at the Philmont Training Center and wanted to take my mother, my sister Jorji, and me.

Like many other teens that have received that news, my 13-year-old mind was starting to lose its desire to go anywhere with my parents, especially on a trip that involved driving from Florida to New Mexico to go to a Boy Scout camp.

Little did I know that that trip would be the beginning of a lifetime connection to Philmont and the Philmont Training Center – for all of my family.

To do something that has such a profound impact on Scouting throughout the country – and the world – and on so many families was incredibly rewarding. Every week I watched Scouters and family members enjoy the facilities, the program, the staff, and each other. I often received letters or calls from Scouters who told me that the PTC experience strengthened their family, motivated them to continue in Scouting, or repaired a relationship.

Every summer I was able to meet some of the top Scouting leaders in the BSA and the world. I was also able to work directly with some of the finest people in the world – the PTC staff and faculty.

I think about PTC and the people I worked with there every day. I believe that whatever success I had as the director of the Training Center was due to the support of my family, my understanding of the value of what was happening at PTC, my love for the ranch itself, and most of all the great staff.

There is a sadness that has passed over me nearly every time I have left the Ranch since that first visit in 1971. I always think that it might be my last. As I pass the Villa, look over my shoulder at the Arrowhead Rock on the back side of Tooth Ridge, and on the drive towards Raton or Springer, I reflect on my latest experience and the generosity of Waite Phillips.

Thankfully, things keep happening to draw me back. I hope that continues.

I have always been convinced that, if we use it, the Philmont Training Center can be a tool that will help make Scouting more successful by providing councils, districts, and units with understanding, motivated volunteers – and professionals. It has impacted my life as a son, a Scout, a husband and father, a volunteer, and a professional.

I also hope the Philmont Training Center has had, or will soon have, a positive impact on your life too. I am blessed that I had a chance to be a part of its history, and that I had this chance to share it with you.

Acknowledgements

This project was proposed to me at the Top Hands Conference in August 2005. I was sharing some background on PTC and someone - I wish I could remember who - said "you ought to write a book." Probably to shut me up.

I thought about it for a bit, unsure if I could find enough information, and enough time, to come up with the thoughts behind the formative days of PTC. I happened to be attending the National Outdoor Program Seminar at Philmont that October so I was able to visit with Villa Superintendent Nancy Klein and search through the Villa and Philmont Museum records. As I read through those records, and especially Waite Phillips' and Arthur Schuck's letters, I was amazed at their wisdom and discovered more than enough to get started. Thank you Nancy for your help, your wisdom, and support for me and this project!

When I returned to Kennewick, I found that one of the former Scout executives in the Blue Mountain Council, Phil Robbins, had kept all of his old professional newsletters, Annual Reports to Congress, and *Scouting* and *Boys' Life* magazines dating back to the '40s in boxes stored in the service center. Thank you Mary Ann Price for all of your help in wading through countless magazines and other written materials for anything about Philmont.

Thank you also to: Amber Abercrombie for your wonderful blog. To Don Adkins for information about the South Central Region conferences and his PTC experience. To Dave Bates for the thoughts about your many years at Philmont and suggestions about who I should talk to. To Ken Davis, a former PTC staffer and great Scouter for your advice, contacts, and recollections. To Brian Gray for your friendship, your support of my family, and access to records and your staff. To Dan Zaccara for your encouragement, ideas, thoughts, and for sharing my enthusiasm as I was finding new things that first week of discovery in the Museum. To Jon Halter and Scott Daniels for editorial advice and the support of *Scouting* magazine. To John Henson, another long-time PTC staffer, for your recollections. To Seth McFarland at the Philmont Museum. To Ed Pease for your friendship, support, and for making this possible at all. To Randy Saunders for your help with things I needed there at the ranch when I could not figure out an excuse to visit. To Doug and Sara Seaborne who helped me locate old letters and brochures about PTC. To Warren Smith who was the main editor, and as another "old" PTC staffer, provided important advice, contacts, and recollections. To Bill Spice who made my direct connection with Philmont possible and was a great source of support and information. To Tommy Thomas, who as a staffer in the '50s, a conference coordinator in the '90s, and a dear friend, was a great source of information. To Mark Warren, who was the first editor of all the early chapters and a member of my staff at PTC. To Andrea (Nuccio) Watson who was also an early editor and as a program director at PTC and a member of my staff in Kennewick, was subjected to, and the source of, ideas almost constantly. To Greg Gamewell and Rachel Ricklefs for their ideas. And of course to the Philmont Staff Association who brought this dream to reality, and to my family who tolerated it all - the writing and the years at Philmont.

Bibliography

BOOKS

Huffman, Minor S. *High Adventure Among the Magic Mountains.* Allendale, New Jersey: TIBS, INC., 1988

Murphy, Lawrence R. *Philmont: A History of New Mexico's Cimarron Country.* Albuquerque: University of New Mexico Press, 1972

Phillips, Waite. *Epigrams.* Edited by Elliott W. Phillips. Privately printed, 1964

Wallis, Michael. *Beyond the Hills: The Journey of Waite Phillips.* Oklahoma City: Oklahoma Heritage Association, 1995.

Zimmer, Stephen and Larry Walker. *Philmont: A Brief History of the New Mexico Scout Ranch.* Santa Fe, New Mexico: Sunstone Press, 2000.

Zimmer, Stephen and Nancy Klein. *Vision, Grace and Generosity: The Story of Waite and Genevieve Phillips and the Philmont Ranch.* Cimarron, New Mexico: Boy Scouts of America, Philmont Scout Ranch, 2002

The Philmont Story. New Brunswick, New Jersey: Boy Scouts of America. 1958

ARTICLES

"The Scout Field: Philmont Scout Ranch " Scouting January 1942: 19

"Training at Philmont and Schiff" Scouting May 1951: 2-3

"Scouting the Country: Philmont Vacation" Scouting June/July 1951: 6

"Cub Scouters Pioneer at Philmont" Scouting November 1951: 7

"Family Vacation and Scouter Training at Philmont" Scouting December 1951: 4

"National Conference of Cub Scout Leaders" Scouting January 1952: 13

"Tell 'Em You'll Be There" Scouting January 1952: 24-25

"Leadership At Two National Training Centers" Scouting February 1953: 6-7

"Like a Vacation?" Scouting April 1953: 4

"Scouters Have Fun Too!" Scouting October 1953: 4-5

"It Pays to Go West" Scouting April 1954: 13

Moise, Jim. "Mom Goes to Philmont" Scouting January 1955: 12-13

"Our Family Enjoyed Philmont" Scouting May-June 1955: 19

Schweiker, Maxine. "We Found Scouting's Heart" Scouting January 1958: 4-5

Zimmerman, Josephine S. "Hey Wives! Be Queen for a Week" Scouting February 1962: 12-13, 28

Darvas, Elaine. "Philmont Honeymoon" Scouting. January 1965: 22

"...More Training at Philmont" The Scout Executive June 28, 1968

"NEI Dates at Philmont" The Scout Executive July 12, 1968

"Meanwhile Back at the Ranch" The Scout Executive – National Training Conference Edition August 30, 1968

"Training Center Changes" The Scout Executive November 1, 1968

"Philmont Volunteer Training Conferences" The Scout Executive October 17, 1969
"National Volunteer Training in 1969 " Scouting January 1969: 21
"Philmont Volunteer Training Conferences" The Scout Executive October 17, 1969
"Revised '71 NEI Schedule " The Scout Executive November 13, 1971
Doclar, Ernest. "Philmont The Place to Go" Scouting January-February 1990: 28-30
Steg, Cathleen Ann. "A Family at Philmont" Scouting January-February 1997: 18-21, 39

CORRESPONDENCE (Philmont Museum Collection, Cimarron, New Mexico)
Bullock, George. Letter to Waite Phillips. November 5, 1949
Hill, F. E. Letter to Waite Phillips. September 27, 1949
Phillips, Waite. Letters to Walter Head. November 19, 1941, December 5, 1941, December 11, 1941
Phillips, Waite. Letters to Arthur Schuck. January 28, 1942, February 28, 1949, April 28, 1949, May 6, 1949, July 5, 1949, November 16, 1951
Phillips, Waite. Letter to George Bullock. October 25, 1949
Schuck, Arthur. Letters to Waite Phillips. September 26, 1949, April 15, 1949, April 29, 1949, February 24, 1949, November 24, 1950, May 18, 1950, September 29, 1950, December 26, 1951
West, James E. Telegram to Waite Phillips. December 19, 1941

INTERVIEWS
Littrell, William C. The Philmont Story interview transcript. Philmont Museum. Undated
Bates, David. Personal interview. 2007
Thomas, Ernest R. Telephone and personal interviews. 2005-2008
Adkins, Donald. Personal interview. 2007
Henson, John. Personal interview. 2007
Spice, G. W. Telephone and personal interviews. 2009
Love, Lou. Telephone interview. 2009

MEETING NOTES AND MINUTES (Philmont Museum Collection, Cimarron, New Mexico)
Phillips, Waite. Meeting with Arthur Schuck. March 1, 1949
Phillips, Waite. Meeting with Arthur Schuck. September 28, 1950
Schuck, Arthur. Director of Operations Check Out Report. 1943
Schuck, Arthur. Chief Scout Executive's Report to Executive Board. October 20, 1949
Schuck, Arthur. Meeting with Waite Phillips. September 16, 1950
Boy Scouts of America. Report of the Finance Committee. Excerpts from Minutes of the Executive Board. December 18, 1941
Philmont Scout Ranch. Ranch Committee Minutes. September 19, 1974
Philmont Scout Ranch. Ranch Committee Minutes. February 24, 1976

ANNUAL REPORTS
United States. 82nd Congress, 1st Session, House Document No. 97. 41st Annual

Report of the Boy Scouts of America 1950. GPO, 1951

United States. 83rd Congress, 1st Session, House Document No. 112. 43rd Annual Report of the Boy Scouts of America 1952. GPO, 1953

United States. 83rd Congress, 2nd Session, House Document No. 356. 44th Annual Report of the Boy Scouts of America 1953. GPO, 1954

United States. 84th Congress, 1st Session, House Document No. 110. Boy Scouts of America 45th Annual Report 1954. GPO, 1955

United States. 84th Congress, 2nd Session, House Document No. 367. 46th Annual Report of the Boy Scouts of America 1955. GPO, 1956

United States. 85th Congress, 1st Session, House Document No. 141. 47th Annual Report of the Boy Scouts of America 1956. GPO, 1957

United States. 85th Congress, 2nd Session, House Document No. 353. 48th Annual Report to Congress Boy Scouts of America 1957. GPO, 1958

United States. 87th Congress, 1st Session, House Document No. 119. 51st Annual Report Boy Scouts of America 1960. GPO, 1961

United States. 88th Congress, 2nd Session, House Document No. 241. 54th Annual Report to Congress, Boy Scouts of America 1963. GPO, 1964

United States. 89th Congress, 2nd Session, House Document No. 410. 56th Annual Report to Congress, Boy Scouts of America 1965. GPO, 1966

United States. 91st Congress, 1st Session, House Document No. 87. 59th Annual Report to Congress, Boy Scouts of America 1968. GPO, 1969

United States. 92nd Congress, 2nd Session, House Document No. 92-263. Boy Scouts of America Annual Report to Congress 1971. GPO, 1972

Boy Scouts of America. Boy Scouts of America 1977 Annual Report to the 95th Congress, 2nd Session. North Brunswick, New Jersey, 1978

BROCHURES AND PAMPHLETS

Philturn Rockymountain Scout Camp. Boy Scouts of America. 1939

Philturn Rockymountain Scout Camp. Boy Scouts of America. 1940

As Philmont Goes. Boy Scouts of America. 1947

Junior Leader Training at Philmont. Boy Scouts of America. 1949

Hi Scouters! Training For You and a Vacation for Your Family. Philmont Scout Ranch. 1953

1957 Volunteer Training Center. Philmont Scout Ranch. 1956

Family Guidebook. Philmont Training Center. 1996

BLOG

Abercrombie, Amber. The Abercronicles. "Country That I Love" May 9, 2009.

Index